affect destiny

THE
BOOK OF HOPE
STORY

BOB & ROB HOSKINS

WITH JAXN ARONNAX-HILL

Other books by Bob Hoskins
The Middle East and the Third World War
The World's Greatest Need
Winning the Race for Russia
Study War No More
All They Want is the Truth

Other books by Rob Hoskins
Then ... Seeds of Spiritual Lineage

ISBN 1-931940-75-4

Cover and Interior Design: J. David Ford & Associates
www.jdavidford.com

Book of Hope
3111 SW 10th Street
Pompano, FL 33069
1-800-GIV-BIBL (448-2425)
info@bookofhope.net
www.bookofhope.net

Book of Hope UK
P. O. Box 6558
Oldbury
West Midlands
B69 4JP
0121 601 6678
david.lherroux@virgin.net

Table of Contents

Chapter
One

L et me take you back, oh my goodness, quite a few years, when little Bobby Hoskins was just seven years old, to the day I received a vision of Jesus. After a Sunday morning church service, I spent six hours with the Savior. During this time God showed me the lost souls of generations, from around the world. As far as the eye could see, it was an ocean of lost humanity. It seemed numberless, infinite, and I remember crying out to Jesus, "How can we ever reach them all?"

After this time, I knew what the course of my life would be. I had been called to win souls to Jesus. I started right away. My parents helped me take to the evangelistic field where, as a seven-year-old child, I began preaching my first sermons.

As I grew up, I kept preaching. When I married my wife Hazel, our honeymoon was our first missions journey to Africa, and from there we went around the world, sharing the good news of Jesus. We lived for more than a decade as missionaries in the Middle East, raising two young sons and a baby girl. We had gone there with the vision to launch the first Christian television program in the Arabic world, and we even got as far as our first broadcast. The response to the program was so overwhelming — so many Muslims wrote and called asking for more information about Jesus — that it made the local authorities nervous, and they canceled our permit to broadcast.

That was quite a blow to me and Hazel, for this was our reason to be in the Middle East, but God quickly revealed to me another reason. Although I could not publicly preach the good news and launch new churches, I could send Arabic-language literature through the mail. With little advertisements in local newspapers, we offered free religious study materials, and an immense correspondence ministry called *Way to Life* was launched. Over 450,000 students enrolled in 22 Arabic-speaking countries in just 15 years. It grew very rapidly and impacted thousands across the Muslim world. After considerable violence and our home being bombed, my presence became more of a hindrance to *Way to Life* than a help because of the opposition to our work, so Hazel and I reluctantly packed up our kids and our things and moved on.

But God had taught me a wonderful lesson: where missionaries cannot go, and where TV broadcasts cannot reach, the printed page *can* go and make a wonderful difference. When I was appointed president of the Gospel publishing house called Life Publishers, I was convinced that I would be able to continue fulfilling the mandate God laid on my heart all those years ago through the power of the printed page. This work was fulfilling. We were providing translations of Bibles and important Christian works in many languages, and I dared to dream that this might even be my final job, the place I could call my ministry home until God called me home.

In 1987, during a time of fasting and prayer, God again showed me horrible scenes of how Satan was going to unleash the greatest spiritual attack this planet had ever known—that he was going to unleash all of his hellish powers to destroy an entire generation. I saw him specifically releasing demons to target the children and young people for destruction. Through poverty and famine, through violence and war, through the proliferation of alcohol, drugs, and sexual permissiveness, with the accompanying diseases like AIDS, Satan would try to wipe out an entire generation. As these horrible scenes of death and carnage unfolded before me, for days I was weeping and crying, "God what are you saying? What does this mean? What am I to do?"

I was overwhelmed by a burden I didn't understand, and in some strange way it seemed connected with children. I like children — I adored my own boys, and my daughter, and I loved the little grandbabies Hazel and I had. But this was something different. I would see a report on the news about suffering children, and I would begin to sob. It got so bad that when I saw kids eating with their folks in a restaurant, or just playing on a playground, my eyes would fill with tears. It was as if all I could see when I saw children were their little lost souls, doomed to hell. At night when I closed my eyes and tried to sleep, all I could see were the faces of children, impressed on my mind and heart.

As I cried out to God for an answer to what this was all about, He spoke, "The only thing that overcomes lies is truth. My Word is truth. I want you to take My Word to the youth and children of the world, and you will do it through leaders."

I asked my good friend and ministry partner, Dr. Dale Berkey, to pray with me about this burden, and as he and I sought the Lord together in an intense time of prayer, the message became clear: God wanted us to take His Word to the children of the world, and He would open doors through world leaders.

I knew what God meant by His Word; I knew what He meant by children; I wasn't sure what He meant by leaders. Since we were the largest publisher of Christian material in several languages, including the Spanish language, I decided to start with leaders in Spanish- speaking nations of the world. We got the names of the fifty most powerful leaders in every Spanish-speaking country — presidents, vice-presidents, heads of education and the military, and business people — and I had their names embossed in gold on one of our beautiful leather Spanish study Bibles. We sent these Bibles out with a message commending God's Word as a map for their lives and as a guide for their nations.

The response was incredible. Within weeks, I was receiving response from leaders across the Latin world. As a result, I was a guest of the presidents of several nations, and had the chance to share with them, personally, the importance of the Word of God.

But the most remarkable response came from the country of El Salvador, where the Minister of Education wrote to thank me for the Bible and then went on to describe the horrible civil war that was tearing his nation apart. He said that it was the children that were suffering the most; their hope and their future had been stolen. He asked if it was possible for us to provide Bibles for all the children in all the schools of El Salvador.

Imagine my excitement! I responded immediately with a great big "yes!" not even knowing how many children there were or where I would get the Bibles to provide them.

After I had sent him my enthusiastic response, I thought to turn to my secretary and ask, "How many schoolchildren are there in El Salvador?"

It turned out that there were close to one million. Maybe I should have asked that before I sent the telegram, but too late now. One million children would be counting on us to give them God's Word. So what should we give them? A Bible would be nice, and they could probably read an age-appropriate Bible, starting in Genesis, with "God created the heavens and the earth." That part is great. But Adam's family gets a little dysfunctional with Cain and Abel, and then there is some other stuff in Genesis that I find hard to figure out now as an adult and a minister. How far would little children get with it?

We decided that if we had the one chance to take the Word of God to an entire generation, that we had to give them what was most important: the Gospel of how to be saved. Once we get them into a relationship with Jesus Christ, we decided that then their own local churches can help them study the rest of the Bible. So we teamed up with an educational specialist to harmonize the four Gospels, so that we could tell the life story of Jesus in chronological order, with nothing repeated, but nothing left out. We came up with *El Libro de Vida,* which would become our *Book of Hope.* It told everything in Jesus' story, from his virgin birth in the stable to His teachings and miracles, to His death on the cross and glorious resurrection. We added 100 study questions at the end of the book that directed the students back into the Word, and we made sure the book had a plan of salvation that clearly told children how to accept Christ as Savior.

What happened next was a real miracle of partnership and unity among God's people in the U.S. and in El Salvador. I wrote to all of my friends and told them about this wide open door to help the children of El Salvador. I told them we could print this book and get it to the kids for just 50¢ per child. Meanwhile, missionary John Bueno was organizing the believers of El Salvador. They had agreed to receive the books at the docks when they arrived, and take them to every school across the nation. I immediately heard from two close friends and ministry partners, Chuck Freeman and Jim Holt. These two men (Jim has since gone on to be with the Lord) have been leaders in Light For The Lost, an Assemblies of God organization that provides literature materials for missionaries. When they heard of this incredible opportunity they said, "Go for it! This is what LFTL is all about," and pledged $250,000 in seed money. Others responded with the additional $250,000 needed to reach every child in El Salvador. Our El Salvadoran partners took the books in boxes and baskets, in cars and trucks, on bicycles, donkeys and even balanced on their heads, and trekked them into every school and into the hands of every schoolchild in the nation, from the largest city schools to the tiniest forgotten one-room school houses of the countryside.

I remember so vividly the story of one teacher way out in the countryside who broke down in tears when one of the brothers arrived with the books. "A gift for us?" she cried. "No one ever remembers us out here!"

Further, many of the teachers told the local volunteers, "You can't just give us this book and leave. We don't know anything about it. Why don't you tell the children what is in this book, and explain it to us?" Across El Salvador, the followers of Jesus had an opportunity to stand up in front of classroom after classroom and explain the Gospel of Jesus Christ to the students and teachers. Many times they were even able to lead the children in praying to receive Christ as Savior, right there at school.

The Bible-believing churches of El Salvador began to fill with new believers. We received report after report of children, and their families, committing their lives to Christ because of God's Word in the pages of this little book. Then we should have expected it, but we didn't: a missionary from the island of Haiti called and said, "What are the chances that you can get that book translated into French for Haiti?" Soon, other Spanish-speaking nations were asking for *El Libro de Vida* for their students. It was amazing! Word of this book's potential was racing across Latin America and the Caribbean, and even around the world. When some of the French-speaking nations of Africa heard that the book might be translated into French, they immediately requested it for their schoolchildren.

My son Rob was a grown man by now, a youth pastor in California. He and his youth group were scheduled to go on a missions trip to Honduras, and I convinced him that he could take the *Book of Hope* to the students of Honduras. The doors were opening to so many Spanish-speaking nations, and Honduras was one that had requested the book anyway. So Rob agreed to get his youth group involved in taking the book to the students of Honduras.

Rob and his team presented the *Book of Hope* in a high school with 17,000 students. They began reaching the students in stages, doing assembly after assembly throughout the day. The response was so overwhelming, that school officials asked them to return the next day and continue until they had reached every student with God's Word.

The second day, a young man caught Rob's eye. Just yesterday, he said, he had been dissatisfied and militant, and had joined one of the radical groups that plotted to overthrow the government by violence. But then he had received the *Book of Hope* at one of the assemblies. He took it home and read it through three times! He felt some power in the pages of this book that drained him of his desire for violence and radical rebellion ... instead, he wanted to know Jesus!

Rob had the privilege of leading the boy to Jesus, right there at school. In a moment of time, the poverty, abuse and hopelessness he had lived with all his life fell away, and the Savior brought him into a new life of hope for eternity.

The affect of God's Word was immediate on that young man's life, for it transformed him. But there was an impact on my son, too. Of course, he had grown up hearing about my vision of lost humanity when I was just seven years old. That night, God gave Rob a vision of his own regarding the lost souls of this earth, with its basis in Revelation 22, the beautiful passage where John describes his vision of the holy city, the new Jerusalem. He speaks of the tree of life, with a fruit that is used for the healing of the nations, of a crystal river that flows from the throne of God and the Lamb, of an endless day, where the dark of night never intrudes because of the brightness of our Savior and God the Father.

The Scripture also says that there is a wall around this holy city, and a gate. The saints of God are inside the walls, continuously praising the Lamb, but there is someone outside the walls, too. "... Outside the city will be dogs, witches, immoral people, murderers, idol-worshipers, and everyone who loves to tell lies and do wrong" (Revelation 22:15).

God gave Rob a vision of that holy city — and of those forbidden to come in who are outside the city gates. What Rob saw, that many of us have failed to see when we read that passage, is that *we* are in the city now, because we have Jesus in our hearts. We don't have to wait for that city, because Jesus has already brought us in and allowed us to wash our robes in His blood (Revelation 22:14). But the lost are still on the outside of that city — three billion or more who have either rejected the love of God or have never heard that God loves them. It doesn't matter why they have never accepted Christ, only that they have not.

In our relativistic post-Christian America, we don't like to think about or speak about the fact that plenty of good, law-abiding people are going to hell. We don't like to focus on the fact that all those over the age of accountability — whether they have ever heard of Jesus or not — will go to hell if they do not accept Him as Savior. They are on the outside of the gates of the heavenly city until they, too, wash their robes in the blood of Christ. This is the vision Rob received: a vision of the billions who have either never heard the good news or never accepted it, locked outside the gates of that beautiful city.

After the Bible describes the doomed billions outside those gates, it records the voice of Jesus who says, "I am Jesus! I am the one who sent my angel to tell all of you these things for the churches. I am David's Great Descendant, and I am also the bright and morning star. The Spirit and the bride say, 'Come!' Everyone who hears this should say, 'Come!' If you are thirsty, come! If you want life-giving water, come and take it. It's free!" (Revelation 22:16-17).

Who is Jesus talking to? The Spirit and the bride say, "Come!" *We* are the bride, the church, already safely inside the gates. He is not talking to us. He is talking to the people outside the gates. Jesus is saying that He, Himself, the Holy Spirit, and His bride — the church, us — all want those outside the gates to come in! This is the vision God gave to my son Rob that night. The church must join the Savior in calling to those who are lost, "Come and taste this living water. Come and join us!"

This is the vision of the *Book of Hope*, and this is our mission:

TO AFFECT DESTINY AROUND THE WORLD BY PROVIDING GOD'S ETERNAL WORD TO ALL THE CHILDREN AND YOUTH OF THE WORLD.

Chapter
Two

After the triumphant arrival of the *Book of Hope* in El Salvador, it became a mad rush to see where we could go next with God's Word. Rob was so impacted by his vision and what he had seen in Honduras, that he rapidly became more involved with the ministry, and I, too, found that the *Book of Hope* began to take up an inordinate amount of my time. It became clear that the *Book of Hope* ministry was to be a full-time calling and separate from its important mother ministry, Life Publishers. Although I still cherished the people and products of the larger ministry, it was obvious that God wanted to take the *Book of Hope* to new countries, and that someone else would now be better suited to take over Life Publishers.

God was fulfilling His original promise that we would reach the world's children through world leaders. More and more world leaders were actually calling us, or agreeing to meet with us. I had a meeting with President Pinochet in Chile, and I had a meeting with President Daniel Ortega in Nicaragua. They were impressed with the beautiful Bibles we had sent them, and they wanted to know more. Now I had something to tell them!

Sometimes when people heard who I was meeting with, they would ask, "Would you do that? Would you meet with fascists and communists?" I would tell them, "I'll meet with fascists, I'll meet with communists, I'll even meet with the Supreme Court justices of the USA if it means I can get God's Word into the hands of lost children and youth."

With Rob, my buddy Dale, and our staff, we began to plan for taking the *Book of Hope* to the children of the world. We discovered that if we could translate the existing *Book of Hope* into just ten major languages, we could conceivably reach 60% of the schoolchildren of the world. With just 20 languages, we could reach nearly 90% of the world's schoolchildren.

Suddenly it seemed that we were seeing a reversal of the Tower of Babel: where once God had confused and separated men for their pride and arrogance by dividing people and tribes according to vastly different languages, now He was bringing them together! More and more people were speaking fewer and fewer languages, with the happy result that we could translate God's Word into just 20 major languages and have a children's version of the Scriptures suitable for 90% of the world's schools!

What could stop us? We thought we were pretty good strategists. We set our goals, and we made our list. Have you ever noticed that we make our list, and then God makes His list, and they are rarely the same?

Several years ago, Hazel and I had the opportunity to see a great play in the city of London. It was called *Letter of Resignation*, and it was the story of the infamous Profumo Affair that took place during the prime ministership of Mr. Macmillan. Some of you may recall that the Minister of Defense, a Mr. Profumo, had a sexual relationship with an employee from the Russian Embassy, and it was suspected that she was probably a Russian plant and spy. There was a great furor over such a situation at the height of the Cold War and, of course, Profumo had to resign.

Prime Minister Macmillan was at his country estate and his administrator traveled to the country to deliver Profumo's letter of resignation. According to the play, Macmillan truly liked Profumo and was so saddened by the turn of events. His personal administrator understood this, and so they had a dialogue built around the letter of resignation. It turned out that the administrator was somewhat of an agnostic and Prime Minister Macmillan was known for his strong religious faith. Much of the play is Macmillan really sharing his faith with the administrator. One of the great moments, a moment that describes what I am saying here, comes when Mr. Macmillan asks the administrator, "Do you know what makes God laugh?" And the response is, "I didn't know God laughed!" Mr. Macmillan responds, "Oh, yes He does. God laughs when men make their plans." That's the way it was with our list. We had our list, but God was laughing, because His list went far beyond anything that our wildest imagination could have possibly conjured.

We put all the easy languages at the top of the list: Spanish, French and Portuguese, figuring we could do those, no problem. All the tough ones went way down to the bottom of the list. One day a fellow who was visiting our offices looked at my list, and he said, "You're leaving out millions of children if you don't get Russian on the list." This was the 1980's, and the Soviet Union looked like it would last another 70 years easily. The Iron Curtain seemed as firmly in place as it had ever been, and the last I had heard, it was still a serious crime to smuggle contraband literature into Russia.

I had no problem with those whom God had called to smuggle Bibles. I have had and continue to have nothing but the greatest admiration for people like Brother Andrew. But God had told us that we would go through the front door and that we would reach the children through the leaders, and I saw no possible way that that would happen in Russia, at least in my lifetime.

I told the inquiring friend as much, as though the matter was closed. But a few months later, I was in prayer with some friends, and the Lord told me to put the *Book of Hope* into the Russian language. That was on Friday. On Monday, when I returned to my offices, I had visitors with a shocking inquiry. A wonderful brother from Sweden who had a compassionate ministry to some of the physical needs in the Soviet Union had been given a permit to legally import fifty thousand Bibles. They said they wanted this limited distribution to be evangelistic and wanted to use the *Book of Hope*. I explained that my specific direction was to take it to children and youth, and if ever there were an opportunity to do that in Russia, I would enthusiastically participate. A few months later, they were back with an invitation to accompany them, as special guests of the Soviet government.

Stunned and thrilled, I went to Russia myself with these missionaries, and there I was introduced to the Minister of Education for the Russian Republic, Igor Vischepan. When he heard about the *Book of Hope,* he told me, "You're late, Mr. Hoskins. You're in a race for the souls of the next generation, and you're already losing it. The Mormons are already here. The Moonies are already here. The Hare Krishnas are already here. The Church of Satan is even here. You're late." With that, he gave me permission to bring the *Book of Hope* for every schoolchild in the republic of Russia, at that time 34 million students!

I wasn't ready for that. The walls of Jericho fell while I was still marching around with my trumpet. Seventy years of communist atheism was crumbling, and I wasn't ready. I got ready fast. The call went out to our ministry friends, and they responded with prayers and faithfulness. The *Book of Hope* was carefully translated into Russian, and we sent the first shipments in 1991, just a few months before the fall of the Soviet Union. What a miracle that was. I wish you could have stood beside me in classroom after classroom as I was able to personally share the truth of the Gospel with children and youth who had perhaps never heard of Jesus before, and certainly never heard that He was God and the Son of God.

We had a problem in Russia. We had found in Latin America that the local churches were strong and ready to take the *Book of Hope* and distribute it to the children and in the classrooms on their own. Even in Haiti and some of the nations of Africa where we used the French-language *Book of Hope*, the national believers were able to take charge and make sure every child received it. In Russia, the local churches were small, and the believers had been persecuted for 70 years. They were frightened and unused to trusting anyone except their own small cell of believers. There weren't enough of them to give the *Book of Hope* to all the children in a city, even if they had been willing to do so.

I remember so clearly, a wonderful pastor in St. Petersburg, Russia, at that time still called Leningrad. He had been prominent even during the strong Soviet rule, and he was not afraid to welcome us and the *Book of Hope*. But his church was small. Leningrad was a huge city, and he didn't have nearly enough people in his congregation to send even one person to each school, and most of the schools were far too big for one person to effectively reach every student. He said to me, "You have lots of believers in America. Why don't you send some over here to help us?" Why not? It seemed the perfect solution! I called different pastors and asked if they would be interested in sending a team of volunteers to Russia. What a tremendous response! Over 250 American believers joyfully came to Russia for the "invasion" of Leningrad!

We broke them into teams of 3-4 people. Each one had an interpreter either from the church or someone we had hired to go with them. The Russian children and teenagers loved their new American friends. They were full of questions and wanted to know everything about America and American kids. They wanted to hear American music, see American movies, watch American TV. They were eager to hear whatever these teams had to tell them, and virtually everywhere the Americans went, they were surrounded by Russian boys and girls who wanted their autograph or their address so they could correspond.

And it wasn't the children only who poured their love out on the Americans. The schoolteachers and principals, the family members, moms, dads and grandmas and grandpas did, too. They brought little gifts, gave them treats from their own meager food resources, and invited the team members into their homes. Their love was returned by the teams, too, who suddenly realized: while the Soviet Union may have been an evil empire, the Russian people were wonderful, caring souls.

St. Petersburg was a great victory for the *Book of Hope*, especially because it opened a new door of ministry for us: volunteer Affect Destiny Teams to help get distribution started. Soon the teams became a staple for the ministry in Russia, even helping to launch new churches. The teams began to serve a distinct purpose, and they developed into one of the foundations of our ministry in Russia, or in any nation where the local believers need help either in numbers or in learning how to coordinate the distribution and bring new believers into the church. We soon began organizing citywide Hope Fest crusades in conjunction with the *Book of Hope* distribution, and our volunteer teams were a huge help with this.

I remember one volunteer who was happy to be there, happy to carry boxes of books, happy to stand back behind the other two team members as they gave their testimonies, and happy to give the book to the kids and shake their hands. But when it came to saying anything aloud, directly speaking in the front of the classroom to the whole class, he was shy, a little nervous, and convinced that if he tried to speak to a group, he would say something dumb. Then, the unthinkable happened! One school was so big that they asked the team to split up, and they sent each American with one of the English-speaking teachers, so they could reach more classes at once. He was going to have to speak to the kids. In the few minutes as he was hurried to the classroom, he prayed that God would give him the words …

… and God did! His testimony story was short, heart-felt and a great success with the students! When he was reunited with the two ladies that made up his team, they were astounded to hear how joyful he was that he had been forced to speak. From that day on, he wanted to be the one to make the presentation and speak to the class, because he knew God was going to give him just the right words to introduce Jesus.

God used Affect Destiny Teams in Russia in remarkable ways. Often churches would send a team of teenagers, or a Bible college would send a team of students, and these volunteers were always very welcome wherever they went. They began to present school-wide assemblies in place of individual classroom presentations, with drama, music, and a young person sharing a personal testimony of God's life-transforming power. The Russian students loved these presentations so much that when the teams then invited them to Hope Fest crusades, they were anxious to come and hear more.

Today, Affect Destiny Teams still fulfill these same basic functions, but now, more and more local churches are sending the teams, rather than relying on Americans. This is a great tribute to our underlying principle of working directly with the national church. In any new area when a door opens, we immediately interface and partner with national believers. We partner with any Bible-believing church that is ready and willing to bring young people and children into the kingdom. We steer the children and families we reach toward the local churches where they can be discipled and grow in the faith. Jesus promised to build His church, and so our idea is to get every boy and girl into a growing church.

Miriam Machovec was another of the believers who made that first Affect Destiny Team mission to Russia. Miriam says she used to read the Bible and knew that Jesus commanded us to take the Gospel to the world, but before 1988, she thought it must be some kind of mistake. She did not see how it would be possible for us ever to reach every nation with the Gospel. In 1988, she heard about the *Book of Hope*, and our ambitious plan to give God's Word to the next generation. Hearing that, she says, made her think, "There is a light at the end of the tunnel. Maybe we *can* do this."

Miriam was so impressed with the ministry and her experience in Russia that she wanted to help us organize more American teams. Or at least she felt that we needed her help to organize more teams. She says, "They wanted to start this ministry of sending teams, and they had no budget for it. I was praying, 'God, you have to send someone down there to help.' Then I heard a voice in my head: 'What about me?' And I thought, 'Yes, I could go.'"

In October of 1991, Miriam moved to south Florida near the Book of Hope ministry center and began helping me organize volunteer teams to take the *Book of Hope* to the children. From that day to this, Miriam has been indispensable to the ministry here, doing whatever we've asked her to do, and doing it well. She has been in several nations around the world with various teams. She works with women's ministries, seniors' ministries, children's ministries, and helps to get more and more people like herself involved in this movement, the movement to preach the Gospel to every child and youth.

She says, "I have a passion to reach the lost, and I can't think of anything I would rather be doing. While I am living far from my own grandchildren, I know that I am reaching someone else's grandchildren with the good news about Jesus."

Another believer who came to Russia and took what she learned there seriously was Marilyn Baughman. A young boy in Russia asked her, "Do you hand out this book to students in America?" Marilyn had to say no. But then she got to thinking: "Why not?" She went home, did some research, and discovered something. Students at any public school that has any extra-curricular clubs on campus have a right to organize a Bible club and bring their literature onto campus and hand it out.

That means that believers who organize into a Bible club at any public school that has other clubs can give the *Book of Hope* to their classmates, right at school! Marilyn spear-headed the project of developing the *Book of Hope USA* for the schools here, designed to speak to the felt needs of American youth and bring them to Jesus. Today, this campus ministry is active in many cities across the United States and is ever-expanding. The Scripture is back on campus, thanks to Marilyn and her determination to obey the call of Christ when he commanded her to spread the light in the schools of the U.S.

In fact, my granddaughter Diandra was recently part of the *Book of Hope USA* distribution in Broward County, Florida, where we live. What a thrill it was, having seen this life-changing book distributed to students in over 120 nations around the world, to see it here firsthand reaching kids right in my own backyard. Thanks to God's immutable power, it can happen here, across the USA, and around the world.

In Russia, for a short time, we had carte blanche to distribute the Word of God in the schools. Satan is not omniscient, and he is not omnipotent. He is powerful, and he has intelligence, but he is no match for our God. I believe he was caught as totally unaware as I was when the Iron Curtain fell in Russia. He had been ruling through atheistic Soviet communism for 70 years, and I believe he thought he would see at least another 70 years of his evil rule. When God brought down the curtain, Satan was caught napping as surely as we were. I believe that is part of the reason our initial distribution of the *Book of Hope* made such a huge impact in Russia. Satan didn't have the time to organize a resistance to us. For a wild couple of years, we were heroes wherever we went, and the dear Russian people received and accepted the hope and light we brought to them.

But Jesus told a story that prepared us for what happens when Satan is ousted, and then has a chance to regroup. "When an evil spirit leaves a person, it travels through the desert, looking for a place to rest. But when it doesn't find a place, it says, 'I will go back to the home I left.' When it gets there and finds the place clean and fixed up, it goes off and finds seven other evil spirits even worse than itself. They all come and make their home there, and that person ends up in worse shape than before" (Luke 11:24-26).

Who can say but that this has been the pattern in the former USSR? When the evil of the atheistic communist system was driven out, churches and missions organizations came in with a clean-up operation that launched new churches, distributed Bibles and literature, and proclaimed the Gospel of Jesus, often primarily in the big cities. Other ministries, like Book of Hope, pressed out of the big cities when we saw that they would be well tended to by other organizations, and began going to the smaller towns, regional centers, and villages. We made contacts with the local school boards, developed a reputation for integrity and helpfulness, and partnered with local churches and believers, so that we became well accepted by local city governments and education boards. While we were busy expanding, Satan wasn't idle. He was casting about for something seven times worse than what he had already subjected the Soviet Union to. What did he find?

First, he found drugs and crime. The Soviet state had so

tightly controlled every aspect of Soviet life that illegal drugs and the high-dollar morally bankrupt criminals in the drug industry had been unable to find a foothold and a nationwide outlet for their product. When the state's mighty machine of control fell, Satan rushed in with narcotics and criminal gangs. The old system was corrupt, without doubt. Without any government checks and balances, the corruption ran amok and whole sectors of large cities fell under the control of brutal new Russian mafias. Marijuana, cocaine, heroin and other drugs became as readily available as they are in the U.S.A. Sad to say, Russians already had a problem with alcoholism. Statistics suggest that fully 30% of Russian men and at least 15% of Russian women are alcoholics. And the annual death toll in Russia from "alcohol poisoning" alone (that is drinking so much so quickly that the alcohol becomes toxic and kills you) is 35,000, compared to about 300 in the USA — and that doesn't count the millions of alcohol-related deaths brought about by disease, drunken driving and the like.

Cheap local vodka is sold in Russia with a pull-away plastic seal that can't be resealed, the assumption being that the entire bottle will be consumed at one sitting. Alcohol has long been the drug of choice for Russians who couldn't cope with the hard realities of life under Soviet rule. When young people already conditioned to drink their troubles away were given the opportunity to blast them away on a rocket-powered heroin high, they were all too willing to accept.

Then there was obscenity and immorality on a scale previously forbidden in the Soviet Union. While the devil used communist atheism to keep people from God in the former USSR, he had to put up with its necessary lip service to the rights and empowerment of women and the importance of hard work and right living. Prostitution, pornography and homosexual activity were all against the law under the old Soviet system, and the state-sponsored censors strictly regulated what kind of movies and books were available to the public. When that censorship was dropped due to the fall of the Iron Curtain, obscenity and immorality rushed in to fill the void very quickly. Prostitution became an accepted line of work for Russian women and girls. Pornography appeared on every street corner.

And western movies that glorified sex and violence were hungrily devoured in Russia. Gay bars and homosexuality, too, came out of the closet.

It was so shocking, just a couple years after we first began to minister in Russia, to read the sad statistic that in a nationwide poll, prostitution was ranked as one of the most desirable careers by Russia's teenage girls. Their communist training had given them no moral or ethical foundation to discourage using their bodies in that fashion. They could see all around them that the high-class call-girls servicing Russia's *nouveau riche* and wealthy foreign visitors were making far more money than any other career women in Russia, so they dreamed of taking up that profession, too. Although communism's design had been to empower women as workers, in Russia it had also somehow stripped them of the idea of respect for their bodies as part of respect for themselves.

Under the USSR, religion in all its forms was discouraged. So when the Iron Curtain fell, Satan also struck back with all kinds of religion and metaphysics. Within just a few years of the dissolution of the Soviet Union, the most popular TV show on Russian television was the astrology forecast. Russians had never indulged in anything like that before, and they couldn't get enough of it! Eastern religions and cults like the Moonies and Hare Krishna began to flourish. And in the southern republics of Russia, the sword of Islam began to cut its swath northward from Moslem border nations such as Afghanistan.

War, too, descended on the various republics of the defunct Soviet Union. In the republic of Georgia, there is fighting and civil war. Chechnya demanded its own Muslim state and has been at war ever since. And should other Muslim areas follow suit, smaller republics within Russia could take up their own cries for independence, too.

Sickness and industrial disease manifested in Russia and the other republics, too, although to be fair, Satan had been planning these down through the years. The Soviet Union fueled its military might with factories that had no safety codes and no program for environmentalism. Pollution of the land, water and air was ignored. The result is an inordinately high amount of birth defects, respiratory problems, blood diseases, and cancers — mostly in children, the easiest target, but also in adults. It's not just Chernobyl, although the aftermath of the horrible incident there is still in effect, but the effects are also seen in other cities where traditional power plants and coal consumption were allowed to blight the air and water.

The devil leveled all these attacks at the people of the former Soviet Union, and we challenged them all with the power of God's Word and the light of His love. But every inch of ground we gain for the Gospel — whether in the former Soviet Union, in Asia, Africa, or beyond — is bought through prayer, through spiritual warfare that can only be waged through prayer.

My son Rob is now the executive director of the Book of Hope ministry, and he tells the story of a team he led to bring the *Book of Hope* to one fairly large Russian community, and it seemed a devilish spirit of resistance met them at every turn. The team arrived to give the books in school to the children, but the books did not arrive. They were delayed somewhere along the way. Then as one of the team members negotiated the treacherous Russian streets, a little child jumped out in front of his car. He struck the boy, and the youngster died in this tragic accident. The city government seemed on the verge of rescinding their permission to take the *Book of Hope* into the schools at all, and Rob's heart was breaking. He prayed, "God, I don't understand what is happening. Here we have come with the gift of Life for the children of this city, and somehow we have been involved in an accident that took the life of one of the very people we are trying to reach! What can we do now, God? How can we make this ministry happen?" It was all out of his power, and the only thing really left for him to do was pray.

He called the team leaders to meet him in his hotel room, a room several floors above the ground floor, with a window looking out over the entire city. "I don't know what it is, I don't know what this powerful resistance is, but we have to break it here and now," he told them. "Will you pray with me for this city?"

The team leaders were American pastors, each one having led a volunteer team from their churches to be there and help the local Christians get the *Book of Hope* to the children. Together the men began to pray for God to break the strangle-hold Satan had on the city. They prayed for the children of the city, for their families, for the teachers, and for the principals of the schools. They prayed for the city government, and for an open door to take God's Word to the children and meet them at their point of need. They cried and wept before God, and called on His power to rescue what seemed like a doomed effort to get His Word to the students and their parents.

Some time later, when the praying finally slowed, and then stopped, Rob looked up to see a couple of mystified hotel maids in the room with them, with tears shining in their eyes. "What are you doing?" they asked timidly. "What was that all about?" With the help of some Russian brothers, Rob told these hotel chambermaids that they were praying for the city, because they believed Jesus loved this city and all the people in it. Then they explained who Jesus is, and both the maids made a commitment to Christ. From that moment, it seemed, the resistance fizzled.

Satan is like a roaring lion, the Bible says. He is strong and powerful, seeking whom he may devour. But our prayers shut the jaws of the lion and break the back of his power. Everywhere around the world, Satan fights for the souls of children, and he fights hard. Why this warfare against innocents? First, because Satan is evil, and he hates the children. Second, because Satan knows if he can keep children from coming to Christ, they are less and less likely to do so the older they get. The statistics used to say that 85% of all adult Christians report making a commitment to Jesus before age 18, but nowadays that number has been revised — most people who come to Christ make their decision to live for Jesus by age 14. Children are the most open-hearted, the most available to the Gospel, so they are Satan's target.

Chapter
Three

Vladimir was a boy from Krasnoyarsk, Siberia, who was affectionately nicknamed Volodya. He was a good boy, a real sports fanatic back in the days before the fall of the old Soviet Union. Back then, the USSR was dedicated to training super human athletes and showing them off at the Olympics. Volodya didn't have dreams of the Olympics, but it wasn't an impossibility. He loved playing soccer with his friends, and of course, hockey. Their local youth center made all this possible, coordinating the teams, and maintaining the playing fields. Volodya was like any other young, healthy, energetic boy. He endured his hours at school just for the reward of the hours he could spend on the playing field!

But then the Iron Curtain fell. The Soviet Union crumbled. Those were just words to Volodya — like most Russians, he had never cared to be called a Soviet anyway: he was a Russian! The thing that bothered him about the dissolution of the Soviet Union was that the funding for the youth center and the organized sports teams dried up.

Even before the fall of the Soviet Union, a lot of Russian men had a drinking problem. Life was hard, and vodka eased their pain. When the Iron Curtain fell, and the weaknesses of the Soviet system were exposed to the western world, we were stunned to see that alcoholism had actually shortened life expectancy statistics for Russian males. Fully 30% of Russian men can be classified as alcoholics. And as we know, alcoholism can pass from one generation to the next.

Truthfully, we don't know Volodya's father, or if he even had a father in the home. But if he looked very far for role models after the fall of the USSR, what he found in Krasnoyarsk may have been a lot of adult men who had already succumbed to alcoholism. He decided to try alcohol at age 14 because he and his friends had too much time on their hands. There was no longer a soccer league, a hockey league, a youth center or a sports club. So the boys he used to play with now turned to crime. They focused their abundant energies on stealing, getting vodka, trying to score drugs, and working their way toward more and more violent crimes.

Volodya's circumstances represent those of millions of kids caught in the trap of drugs, alcohol, gang life and crimes. It's a vicious cycle for kids who don't know Jesus.

But then in 1992, the *Book of Hope* came to Krasnoyarsk. Volodya was not very interested in books and took his home to give to his mother. His little sister, however, was very much intrigued by the book and wanted to attend the Hope Fest crusades in the sports arena downtown. The Russian and American teams had invited all the schoolchildren, but Volodya didn't want to go. His mother made him walk his little sister to the services, and he waited outside for her. If there wasn't a sports event inside, he didn't even want to enter.

Then their auntie, who went to college and could speak English, took a job as a translator for the American teams presenting the program. She hurried over to tell his mother all about it. The team had explained Jesus to her, and she wanted to share it with her family! Soon Volodya's sister, his aunt and his mother had all committed their lives to Christ. Even when the American teams left, they attended a new church that Book of Hope helped to plant in Krasnoyarsk, and they prayed that one day Volodya would come to Christ, too. It was difficult enough just to get him to go to church!

The new church and the home Bible studies were such a strong force in Krasnoyarsk, it was difficult to escape from them. Even some of the boys Volodya knew and used to be good friends with had become Christians. And two years later, Volodya, too, found, in an instant at church, what he had been looking for with his buddies, what he had longed for when he resorted to vodka or drugs. He found the light and power of God's love, the only thing he really needed! Today, 26-year-old Volodya is the pastor of the same church that Book of Hope founded in his city, and he is proudly sending teams of Russian believers to take the Word of God into new cities and plant new churches! Already his church has planted 11 new churches in various regions.

In the first few years that the *Book of Hope* made its way across Russia, a young Ukrainian man was having his own revelation of God's power and light. Edward Grabovenko was a hard-drinking young party guy, and he was on his way out on another bender with the boys when the car they were riding in passed a little country church that Edward remembered from his childhood, and something compelled him to call out to his friends to stop the car. He jumped out and rushed into the church, where the Spirit of God overwhelmed him. He fell down before the altar and committed his life to Christ. What a dramatic transformation Edward experienced! But more was to come. Edward was called to be a missionary to the republic of Russia. As a Ukrainian, he did not have especially warm feelings toward Russia, and when he arrived in the city where he was called to found a new church, Perm, he did not receive especially warm feelings back from his Russian mission field.

But he knew God had called him, and he persevered. Then Book of Hope representatives contacted him and asked if his growing church would like to help distribute the books to the children in the Perm area. Although he was skeptical, Edward agreed that his church would distribute 100,000 books. The response from the children and their families was so overwhelming that the next time Edward saw our representatives, he asked for another *one million books* to give to children in Perm and neighboring cities! Today, Edward's church has grown exponentially, and the believers there have launched nearly 200 new churches with over 30,000 believers throughout their region and beyond, even sending missionaries into Muslim republics of Russia and to minister on the border with Afghanistan. And everywhere they go, they begin with the children, by giving them the *Book of Hope* in their schools and explaining the story of Jesus to them, a story of wonderful power and light. Edward, his New Testament Church, and their daughter churches, have given the *Book of Hope* to over five million children! Praise God! Across the former USSR, over 2,000 new churches have been launched using *Book of Hope* distribution and Hope Fest crusades as their foundation.

Edward's church in Perm, and several other strong and growing churches we have worked with or helped to launch, represent a real revival in Russia, and we are privileged to be part of it. Russia remains a prime example of how the *Book of Hope* can be embraced by the local church and used, not as a missionary tool in the hands of foreigners, but as a real work of evangelism by local believers reaching out to their countrymen. While our American volunteer teams sometimes join the national teams in Russia, more often than not, it is the local believers who deliver God's Word, right to the children, right in their classrooms.

Sasha was another boy whose life was forever transformed by the *Book of Hope* in Russia. He grew up in a Russian orphanage, but by age 16, the juvenile detention center was his home. The poor health-care and hygiene provided for the kids in state custody had left Sasha a victim of tuberculosis, and the beatings he received in juvenile jail left his kidneys permanently damaged and constantly aching.

He was hurting and hopeless by age 16. But then a team of believers, from Pastor Edward's New Testament Church in Perm, arrived at the detention facility to tell the boys about Jesus and give them the *Book of Hope*. Sasha was one of several boys to give his heart to Jesus. Although imprisoned for crimes he had committed as a young boy, he now had true freedom, and hope for eternity in Jesus!

One of the team members, who is now an assistant pastor at the church, continued ministry for the new believers in the juvenile facility. At one of the prison services, God healed Sasha's TB.

When Sasha was released at age 18, his only "family," the New Testament Church, took him in. He slept at the church and served as night watchman, and in the daytime, he listened in on the classes at Bible school and studied on his own, hungry to learn more about the God he now served. During one of the church services, God healed Sasha's kidneys, too.

At age 21, Sasha and students from the Bible school gave every schoolchild in a nearby village the *Book of Hope*, invited all the families to a Hope Fest crusade, and led eight teachers and many students and parents to Jesus. The team has already planted a new church in that tiny village of just 300 families, 70 kilometers from Perm.

Today, the new church has 28 adults and 30 students as members, and Sasha and one of the Bible school students come every weekend to conduct services. God used His Word to reach Sasha, and now is using Sasha to reach others.

Satan attacked Volodya with the temptation of drugs, and ensnared Sasha with crime. But a young lady named Irina had suffered none of that as she grew up in the then-USSR. Satan did not attack her with poverty, for her family was fairly well off by Russian standards of the day. He did not attack her with violence, for the Cold War kept any flesh-and-blood conflict at bay. He did not attack her with substance abuse, for Irina's family was successful and healthy. Nor did the devil attack her with disease or cults — most religion was altogether outlawed, so that was never a threat.

It seems that Satan hadn't attacked Irina at all. Her parents were good people who loved their children, provided well for them, and taught them to behave with respect and honor for themselves and other people. Yet all the same, Irina was barreling down the road toward hell. The Bible says that all have sinned and fall short of God's glory — and that there is only one way back to God: through Jesus Christ. Irina knew nothing of Jesus. What she knew was Communism, Marxism, Lenin and Stalin. After all, as a smart girl from a middle class family, she had been inducted into the Young Pioneers and was a favored member of Komsomol, the youth organization for communism.

She was honored once with a gift from the state as a young lady — a trip to a famous youth camp for communist leaders on the shores of the Black Sea. This was a place for the privileged few who were being groomed to become the communist leaders of tomorrow — not just in the Soviet Union, but in the satellite nations of the communist block, and even in Cuba. Here they would learn how to foment revolution and export communism and Soviet rule to the world.

Irina was surprised and delighted to discover that the girls and boys from Cuba could speak fluent Russian. As they were trained for communist leadership in Cuba, they were also learning to speak the mother tongue of Lenin-style communism — Russian. Together with her new Cuban friends, this young Russian girl walked along the shores of the Black Sea, enjoying the breath-taking scope of the seascape before them, the beautiful scenery around them, and the gorgeous mountains behind them. Someone asked quietly, "Do you believe there is a God?"

The Cuban students seemed undecided. "There must be something beyond all this," they reasoned. But then they turned and looked up into the mountains, where huge letters had been arranged like the famous "Hollywood" sign in California, but these spelled out LENIN. Finally they decided, "There is our God."

It was a moment of relief for Irina! For a few seconds, she had thought they were going to say they believed in God, and for her, that would have been unthinkable! Now that they had correctly identified Lenin as the authority in their lives, she could breathe easy again. She and her friends were in perfect agreement. Religion was a fairy tale, and only what they could accomplish for the party was important.

Although she was a good person and working for the good of her country and family, Irina was just as hopelessly lost and doomed as Volodya, who tried alcohol, or Sasha, who was imprisoned for juvenile crimes. Was Irina any less lost than her Russian brothers? No, all were in desperate need of a Savior, and all were perishing.

Why would they perish? In 2 Thessalonians 2:10, the Apostle Paul says, "They perish because they refused to love the truth and so be saved" (NIV). When Satan gets a free hand to attack the children of unbelievers, he shows no mercy. Poverty, disease, violence, alcoholism, war, cults, and worse. Yet in Soviet Russia, as in middle class America, it didn't take any of that to ensnare and doom a young person like Irina, who was lost not because of the evil she had done, but because she had never embraced the light of Christ.

Irina completed her studies and became a teacher, a job that she loved. But something prompted her one semester simply to quit. For no reason she could think of, she felt it was time to move on. And the next job offer she received was to work as a translator for an Affect Destiny volunteer team from America.

She was intrigued by these Americans. They seemed so *happy*. Well, she decided, they lived in America where life was easy, and no wonder they were happy. But then she noticed something else, something about the Russian believers who were working with the American team. They seemed happy, too! Now why would Russian people be this happy, especially considering that the Soviet system was falling apart around them? Irina listened carefully to the words she was asked to translate daily in the schools for her team, and soon she discovered the secret to their happiness. It was God's love. Time turned a corner, and Irina's communist, atheist roots and upbringing dropped away as if they had never been, and her new future as a child of God unfolded. Communism, atheism, Marxism — these are no barrier to the Word of God.

For Irina, the *Book of Hope* was the catalyst to affect her destiny forever! Today, Irina is the Book of Hope Regional Coordinator for the entire C.I.S.

This is the kind of life-changing, destiny-shaking impact that the *Book of Hope* has upon children and youth in Russia, and around the world. We saw it demonstrated again and again throughout the former Soviet Union in those early days of ministry, and it continues even now.

He had the future of the country in his hands. Sure, he was just teaching kids in a backwater school in one of Russia's myriad small villages, but if there was anything the system taught, it was that anyone could change the course of destiny. Look at the venerated Lenin, the strong man Stalin. They came from nowhere, and forged the future. The children he was teaching today had the same potential to become the communist greats who would lead the Union of Soviet Socialist Republics into a glorious destiny. It was true that just at that moment, millions across Russia and millions more in the other republics of less account were struggling, but the idea of sacrificing comforts and pleasures today in order to build the ultimate state for the workers of tomorrow was ingrained by the Marxist system. He did not mind the sacrifices.

Then one day, ten years into the teaching career that he saw as his small contribution to the state, something happened that changed his life forever. A Bible came into his possession. Yes, such things were available in the USSR, even in the 1970's. They were rare. Usually only university students and teachers had access to them, for the study of the "history of religion." No one took them seriously as divine books dictated by an almighty God ... even to think such a thing was unpatriotic to the extreme. No one knew it better than he did. Year after year, he had seen and heard the presentation of the leader of the Young Pioneers to the first graders. She would come into the classroom and tell the students that today they would study religion, something that was very popular in the decadent United States of America. She would tell them how every day millions of Americans prayed to God in the name of Jesus for their daily needs. What a quaint notion! How would it be, she would ask, if they tried, just for today, what the Americans did every day? What if they prayed to Jesus for something they really wanted — like ice cream!

He knew what was coming. He did not remember it from his own childhood, but something similar must have gone into his communist party training, for he had been a Young Pioneer, too. Everyone of any standing was. The woman would lead the children in a sincere prayer to Jesus for ice cream, and of course, Jesus never sent any ice cream. No one really expected him to. "Why, Jesus must not care much about you children at all," she would say, "if there really is any Jesus. I think there isn't a Jesus or any God either. But I do know someone who cares very much for you! Your country and the communist party care for you. Let's ask the party for ice cream!"

This time, when the children entreated their state party to give them ice cream, the classroom doors opened, and loyal party members brought in a wonderful ice cream treat. From this simple illustration, the students received their first impressions of Jesus, God, prayer and the Bible. They were taught it was all lies.

But then, this Bible. He had this Bible, and he couldn't help but read it. He thought at first it would be interesting just to see what religion and the Bible were all about. But the more he read it, the less he could put it down. And as he read about the life of Jesus, the same strange thoughts kept popping up inside his head. Jesus never rained ice cream down on the school, but he nevertheless had a lot of good ideas. He wanted people to treat each other honestly and kindly. He wanted the sick to be raised to health and their full potential. He wanted his followers to sacrifice for the good of others. These weren't radical ideas. Further, Jesus himself led the way by sacrificing his own life for his friends.

Now the story was really becoming interesting, and as he read of the followers of Christ proclaiming their gospel to their generation, he could not deny the burning desire he felt to be part of this incredible movement of joy and light! Then in the book of Acts when the jailer pleaded with the apostles, "What must I do to be saved?", the words resonated so strongly! *What must I do to be saved?* The Bible clearly told him how to be saved: believe on the Lord Jesus Christ. It was as simple as that, and he did it! The light of God went on inside of him, and he was saved.

How wonderful that a book could bring such a change to his heart. How wonderful that God's Word alone was all that was needed to transform his life!

Of course, he could not share what he had done with anyone. He would lose his job. The state would not allow a follower of Jesus to teach the precious children. He could lose his family. There were tales in years gone by of children seized from their parents because the state judged religious belief to be a mental disease and of parents committed to institutions to medicate the belief out of them. He could not take such chances, so he did the one thing the Bible told him to do. He prayed that one day he would be able to share his faith without fear, and he prayed that the Word of God that had come to him would one day come to the children at his school. He still believed they were the future of his nation, and oh, how he wanted them to learn the truth about Jesus! He knew his prayers would be answered, because the Lord confirmed in his spirit, "One day, someone will bring My Word to the children."

Twenty years later, the USSR was in turmoil. The communist system appeared to be bankrupt, and the ideologies that had held the conglomerate republics together had been weighed in the balances and found wanting. With the economic chaos, the little school seemed to be forgotten by the state. The students did without books and supplies; the teachers did without salaries. He continued to pray, and he looked into the madness around him for the hope and the fulfillment of God's promise. Then one day, he heard that a group of American tourists would visit the school.

That was one of our Affect Destiny Teams that had come to Russia in the first fevered moments of the fall of the

Iron Curtain, to give the students a gift, *Kniga Zhezn,* our *Book of Hope.* As the team stood in front of the school assembly and explained the book and the story of Jesus, they couldn't help but notice the elderly gentleman in the back, tears streaming down his face. They gave each student and teacher a copy of the *Book of Hope,* and afterward the team leader made his way to this Russian man. "I noticed that you were very moved by what we said," the team leader said as they shook hands.

"I have been a teacher at this school for 30 years," the Russian man said. "Twenty years ago, I received a Bible. I read it, and I chose to follow Christ as Savior. I couldn't tell anyone, but every day since then, I have prayed that the children at this school could learn who Jesus really is. God promised me that some day, someone would bring His Word to the children. Today as soon as your team arrived, I saw the light in you, and I knew you were the ones."

Do *you* have the light in you? If you are a believer, you do. And now God has provided a way for that light to touch every single child and youth around the world, fulfilling the Great Commission of our Savior, within our lifetimes. That's what the ministry of the *Book of Hope* is all about, not just in Russia, Latin America, and the USA, but literally around the world.

Chapter
Four

W e were only a few years into the Book of Hope ministry, with new doors opening almost daily, when warfare descended on me in the form of cancer. At the very moment that I wanted to be at my best, my strongest, vital and unflagging, I was knocked down to my knees by a virulent disease that seemed horribly likely to take my life.

I was diagnosed with colon cancer that was already in an advanced stage. If you or a loved one has ever heard such a diagnosis, then you know how I felt, and how my family felt. Cancer is a physical disease, I accept that, but I believe the greatest battle that a child of God wages against cancer is a spiritual battle. Satan was trying to kill me with the disease, but he knew even if he couldn't accomplish that — because Jesus has the keys to death and hell — there was a good chance he could destroy me spiritually with the hideous effects of the surgeries and treatments, and the horrifying mental impact of "the C word."

It is difficult for me now to imagine how anyone could face the prospect of cancer without the love of God to sustain them. Chemotherapy is supposed to cure you ... but its effects can make you wish you were dead. If you did not know that

God loved you and believe with all your heart in Romans 8:28 (all things work together for good) and Jeremiah 29:11 (plans to give you hope and a future), I don't know why or how you could hang on to life during that kind of suffering.

It was during this time that I met another cancer victim (we were both on our way to being cancer survivors!) who told me that she hung onto hope by reminding herself of who she is in Christ. She had gone through verse after verse in the Bible that reflected on what we mean to God, and she proudly labeled herself with each term. We are beloved of God, children of God, healed by His blood, raised by His power, on and on. From her inspiration, we even developed the little booklet *Who I Am in Christ* that has been such an inspiration to so many who are suffering.

But I fully believe that if you are suffering the effects of cancer, treatment for cancer, or another painful or debilitating disease, and your focus is not on Jesus Christ and His power to save, that whether or not you survive the disease physically, you run the risk of being destroyed spiritually. Jesus said the greatest commandment was to love the Lord with all your strength (body), all your heart (soul) and all your mind (intellect). The three are an integrated unit while we live on this earth, and when one suffers, the others suffer as well. Only keeping your heart and mind stayed on Christ can help you pull through a time of physical suffering.

My doctors performed radical surgery to save my life, and thanks to the prayers of God's people, I survived it. When I should have begun to mend, I instead succumbed to a raging infection that seemed to be tearing my insides apart. The doctors couldn't get the infection to respond to any medicines, and the pain was ghastly. The struggle for survival sapped my strength daily. I didn't even have the strength to get out of bed, and eating anything was out of the question. This was worse by far than the suffering with cancer.

The horrible weight of oppression fell onto me under this vicious attack of Satan, and in the natural, physical realm, it seemed obvious that I was on my way out of this life. No one could recover from this virulent an infection so hard on the heels of a drastic surgery. Satan had all but destroyed me physically, but spiritually I was still very much alive, and in the hearts and prayers of my friends, family and partners in ministry, I was still very much alive.

During the spring of 1997, about a year after my surgery, I was still battling cancer, receiving chemotherapy, and wondering what would become of the *Book of Hope*. Then God spoke clearly to me. His message was a surprise ... He said to prepare to double the ministry! I was to put in place the infrastructure that would be needed to double book distribution. By faith I asked the team to put the systems in place, just as if we had the funding to reach twice as many children.

At the same time, God was speaking to a wonderful Christian businessman. This man had a vision to reach the world with the Gospel of Jesus, and He was seeking God's direction for how to do it. God had already made clear to him that there was a divine plan, and that it would be revealed. In May of 1997, this man and his family "just happened" to visit a church where a Book of Hope presentation was being made. When he heard about an economical way to blanket entire cities with the Word, he knew this could be the plan God had spoken of! Within weeks, he and his family asked me to visit them so they could learn more and get involved. Their generous gifts, combined with the generosity of many other friends, enabled us to more than double our outreach.

My heart was rejoicing that God had spoken to me, and to this Christian brother and his family, and made both our visions possible! To this day, the heart of this man, his family and business is in reaching millions of children with the *Book of Hope*.

But my body continued to deteriorate. I was at home dying one Sunday morning, and Rob was preaching in Fort Myers, Florida, at our good friend Dan Betzer's church. People had been praying for me ever since the diagnosis 14 months ago, and I was so grateful for that. Dan decided to lead in prayer for me one more time, and he asked the congregation to stand and sing together God's Word from Scripture, "I am the Lord that healeth thee," but he asked them to substitute my name as they sang, "I am the Lord that healeth Bob." Of course, I didn't know any of this was happening, but there came a moment that Sunday morning when I felt that I might just be able to eat something. I asked Hazel to make me an omelet.

I had been so sick for so long that I hadn't felt like eating anything in weeks, and when I did try to eat, the results were not pretty. Hazel was surprised that I wanted anything, much less an omelet, but she made it for me, and I ate it all. From that very morning, my recovery began. Rob was astounded when he arrived back home! He had been praying for me, friends across the country had been praying for me, and yet I had grown worse and worse. Then, in a moment of time that seemed right to God, I was miraculously healed and restored. God knows that we are under the devil's attack every moment, and He will rescue us in the fullness of time.

Here is how the Apostle Paul described the advent of Christ on earth:

"But when the fullness of time had come, God sent his Son, born of a woman, born under the law, in order to redeem those who were under the law, so that we might receive adoption as children" (Galatians 4:4,5, NRSV).

That sounds beautiful, doesn't it? "The fullness of time had come." I wonder if it sounded that pretty to Mary when the angel announced that God had chosen her to be the vessel of Christ's earthly appearance? After all, it was an honor to be chosen, but the angel was not announcing this choice to the world and publicly crowning her Queen of Heaven so that everyone would know the child she had conceived out of wedlock was the Son of God. No, the whole scenario was quite different.

Imagine how you would feel. Here is a young Hebrew woman, maybe 17 years old, engaged to be married, and she has had a long day, just laid her head down on her pillow, ready to sleep, when all of a sudden a huge angel appears standing in front of her. His greeting confuses her, his appearance frightens her, and he's forced to calm her down. "Don't be afraid," he says immediately. "God is pleased with you." Then he goes on to try to make her feel better by telling her, "You're going to have a baby!" It didn't make her feel better — now she's more frightened than ever.

And Mary is like us. She comes up with the first excuse she can as to why this is impossible. "How can this happen? I'm not married," she says (Luke 1:34). Right away she is thinking, like we always think: "Shouldn't God have chosen someone better qualified then me? How about someone with some child-rearing experience? How about someone who is at least *married*?! You've got the wrong person, God, I'm not the one for this job." Have you ever felt that way?

In fact, today as you read these words, your call from God is much the same as Mary's call. You have been called to birth Jesus into your world, just as Mary was called to birth Him into hers. She was charged with giving physical birth to Him, protecting, nourishing and rearing Him as a child — and you have been called merely to release His light and power into your world, but the call is essentially the same. She brought the Christ-child into the world, and now we must share His glory with our world.

So here is a lesson we can learn from Mary:

1. Understand your call. When the angel explained to her that the Holy Ghost would conceive the child within her, Mary humbly accepted God's call. "I am the Lord's servant," she told the angel. "Let it happen as you have said" (Luke 1:38). Understand and accept the call.

Mary had no reason, other than the angel's message and her own faith in God, to believe that it was time for the Messiah to arrive on earth, but nevertheless, she believed. Most of the religious leaders of her day, the Pharisees, Sadducees, and experienced Hebrew authorities, did not believe the time was ripe for the Messiah and did not recognize Him when He came. They believed that because Israel was under Rome's occupation, with the people dispossessed and no homeland of their own, it could not possibly be the right time for the Messiah. Mary did not bother with all that. She understood that it *was* time, because the angel had revealed as much to her. She understood her times. Do you understand yours?

Never before has any credible religious authority had the audacity to say that their generation can fulfill the Great Commission — but the reason is that never before has any generation had that ability! Even just 20 years ago it still seemed fairly impossible. We didn't have faxes. We didn't have cell phones. We didn't have email, and travel to distant lands was still very expensive and complicated. Today, I can be half a world away from my home on the distant Mongolian edge of Russia, and even there I can instantly communicate with my family and office via email or cell phone. The world is shrinking. And why?

Because God is empowering this generation with the tools we need to bring His light to the four corners of the earth! Believers today need to grasp that now. So here is the second lesson we can learn from the humble and obedient Mary:

> 2. Understand your times. By the end of this book, you will be overawed by your understanding of these times and how God wants you to ride the crest of them to carry His Word to every child and youth in the world. Get ready for that ride!

Once Mary had accepted the angel's message and understood that God wanted to use her to bring His Son into the world, she went to visit her cousin. This seems like a natural thing. The angel had told her that Elizabeth was also expecting a baby, and Mary wanted to share the joy. But I think Mary possibly also wanted confirmation, in a human form she could see and hold onto, of the plan God had set in motion. And as soon as she arrived within sight of Elizabeth, that good woman felt her own baby jump for joy within her womb and called out, "God has blessed you more than any other woman ... The Lord has blessed you because you believed that He will keep His promise" (Luke 1:42,45).

When Mary received confirmation from the lips of Elizabeth of the anointing she already felt upon her and the new life already growing within her, she burst into a joyous song of praise to God. "I am glad because of God my Savior," she sang (Luke 1:47). "From now on, all people will say God has blessed me" (Luke 1:48). Mary understood that the gift she would be allowed to give the world was more important than anything else in her life, or in the world. She understood that in fulfilling the objective God had given her, she would play a role in an eternal blessing for people of all time and eternity.

Sometimes we as believers seem a little mixed up about our anointing. We wait until we receive an anointing to go forward in ministry or in God's work. The problem with that is, the anointing is already on us. Jesus is already in us. The calling has already been delivered to us. If you have accepted Christ as Savior, the anointing abides in you, right now. If you are a follower of Jesus, then you, like Mary, have Christ inside you.

You need not wait for an anointing to fall on you like pixie dust out of the magic wand of an evangelist. The anointing is already resident within you, and you can join Mary in her song: "From now on, all people will say that God has blessed me because He allowed me to fulfill the objective of my life and deliver the Savior to my world."

This then, is another of Mary's lessons for us:

3. Understand your anointing. The anointing we need to deliver Christ to the world is already upon us. And as we understand the times and the technology that have made it possible to fulfill the Great Commission in our lifetime, we can go forward and fulfill that calling — and achieve our destiny!

Chapter
Five

The *Book of Hope* was first given to children in Central America and the Caribbean, and even as Russia and Eastern Europe opened, the Word was continuing to spread in Central and South America. The book had been so well received, in fact, that I was encouraged to request a meeting with President Collar de Mello of Brazil. Our plan was to begin reaching students in Brazil, starting with a section of Sao Paulo city representing about one million schoolchildren. Our research showed that this would be the best jumping-off point because the churches were strong enough to do the leg-work, and because as Brazil's commerce and industry capital, it would be the place to have the most influence in the future. If we could catch these youngsters early with the Gospel, they could grow up to steer the nation toward God.

And because there were only one million students or so, I was confident that we could provide enough books for each one.

President Collar de Mello had been one of the world leaders to receive a gift Bible from us. When we met, I explained the *Book of Hope,* and our desire to bring it first to the students in the Sao Paulo region of Brazil. But there were several other men in the meeting with me and the president, and one of them immediately stood up and said, "If you are giving this book to students in the schools of Sao Paulo, then you must bring it to the schools of Rio as well." Then another weighed in, "The students of Belo Horizonte also deserve this free gift." Finally, it was decided: if we wanted to bring the *Book of Hope* to any of the children of any city in Brazil, we had to bring it to all the children of Brazil.

And there were 32 million of them!

I went home with a heavy heart and cried out to God: "This has gotten out of hand! Thirty-two million students? I could handle it as long as it was a million here or 500,000 there, but 32 million? Where will we get the money for that?"

That's when I heard God say, "Who do you think I am? Do you think I'm such a small God that I am staggered by the idea of 10 million children? Do you think I reach my breaking point at 20 million children? Where do you think I have to draw the line and say, 'That's too many'? This is not your Word that you can dole out to one million children at a time, or half a million at a time. This is not your ministry to keep for yourself or your denomination. This is my Word, and my ministry to the children of the world, for all of them. There is no staggering me! I will provide."

I realized then that as long as we kept our hearts and motives pure before God in this work, finances would not be our problem. I serve a God who owns the cattle on a thousand hills. The Bible says the earth is the Lord's, and the fullness thereof. It says we have title to God's infinite riches in Jesus. God has blessed America's believers in this day and age with unprecedented wealth, and when they choose to pour that wealth back into ministry, finances are no longer a problem. There are enough resources in the pews of our churches to reach the world 10, 20, 30 times over.

Already we have placed the *Book of Hope* into the hands of more than 29 million children and youth throughout various regions in Brazil, and the work continues.

In the South American nation of Peru, the national church warmly responded to the *Book of Hope* and organized to carry it to children in the big cities and small villages, too. I think of Tiffany, a little girl in the slum suburb of Chorrillos on the outskirts of Lima, Peru. Her circumstances exemplify the threat of poverty that hangs over 600 million children who live in extreme poverty (the highest number in history) around the world.

In Peru, a civil war a few decades ago chased hundreds of thousands of peasants from the war-torn countryside into the big cities like Lima, seeking safety from the guerrilla fighting — and of course, seeking jobs and a place to raise their families. Tiffany's parents came in such a wave of refugees from the countryside, and found there was no room for them in Lima. They joined with scores of squatters on a barren, dry-packed patch of dirty hills on the city limits, struggling to construct homes of scraps of wood and stone.

At first they were driven back by the Lima police and authorities who did not want these homeless peasants building a new slum. By sheer dint of numbers, the poor families eventually prevailed, and the government in Lima did what they could for the *campesinos*, in hopes of making the place at least safe. It hadn't ever become safe, but it became sprawling. Houses were slung together with cast-off building materials, and if the family was lucky, a piece of corrugated tin for the roof. By the time Tiffany came along, there were dirt roads through the neighborhoods and even a public school for the children.

Tiffany's mother worked as a maid, for the equivalent of about $40 per month. Her father was an artist, but no one could afford to buy his work. So he spent his days climbing the rough hillsides that surrounded Chorrillos, scouring the dirt for rocks and sticks, then bringing these back down into the still growing slum and trying to sell them as building materials. Tiffany's older sister joined their mother working as a maid, but the family was proudest of elder brother Henry, who was able to attend trade school. He was really their only hope. If they could just keep a roof over their heads and everyone at least halfway nourished until he could graduate and get a real job, maybe there would be a future for all of them. Tiffany's father didn't really believe it. He began drinking in order to dull the pain and despair that he felt.

And nine-year-old Tiffany? She hadn't given in to despair yet. She was still in school, and she still had dreams. She wanted to be a civil engineer and learn to plan better neighborhoods than this one where she lived — she wanted to plan neighborhoods with parks and playgrounds!

She went to school that morning with no particular reason to hope for anything better in the future than what she and her family had experienced in the past: poverty, hunger, hopelessness. But at school she received a special gift from the local church and a visiting team of Americans. It was the *Book of Hope*. In it, she found Jesus, a friend who promised to give her hope and a future! She took the book home and read it through with her sister and her mother. The very next day, Tiffany and her mother both committed their lives to Christ!

Soon, Tiffany's elder sister, brother, and her father also made a commitment to live for Jesus and joined their local church. Although their physical circumstances may not be any better than they were yesterday, suddenly it seems as if the whole landscape has changed. Today, there is hope for eternity.

In Colombia, another little girl also desperately needed hope for the future. Her name was Leide. It's tough for kids growing up in Colombia today, because the entire nation is under the oppression of lawlessness and violence. Assassinations, murder and robbery are commonplace. And Colombia is the kidnapping capital of the world — 50% of all the world's kidnappings take place in Colombia. The violence has its roots in a civil war, the drug cartels, the leftists guerrillas, and the right-wing para-military groups. In Medellin, the latest secret weapon against enemies is teenage assassins. About 5,000 teenagers have already committed murder for hire.

That's where Leide lived, Medellin, and that is the climate of violence in which she was growing up. By age 12, Leide was constantly fighting with her parents and spending more and more time on the streets with her friends — a gang, really, that offered her a place where she felt more needed and loved than she did at home. She was accepted as a friend and part of a pseudo-family among these kids, and she gladly joined in with the gang when they stole from people and spent the money on drugs. Leide quit school, spent less and less time at home, and was soon more or less living on the streets with her gang.

But then when she turned 13, her friends informed her: she had to choose whether she would come all the way into the gang with an important act of loyalty, or leave the gang forever. The gang was her family now. Leide couldn't face the prospect of being abandoned by them! What did she have to do in order to stay with the gang? She would have to kill another teenager, in fact, a good friend. Blinded by her need for the affirmation and closeness of her gang buddies, Leide obeyed them. And at age 13, she became a murderer. She knew there was no going back for her. She felt she had turned her final corner. Although she was allowed to keep her place in the gang, now it brought her little comfort. She abandoned herself totally to the gang lifestyle, because she could no longer feel anything inside.

She threw herself into immoral sexual relationships with boys in the gang. She passed on from petty crimes to violent crimes. She pushed herself deeper into substance abuse and alcohol use. Something that used to be alive in her had died when she killed her friend, and now nothing seemed to matter.

Finally, her parents saw their chance to rescue Leide. They moved their family away from Medellin to the smaller town of Quibdo, and they put Leide back in school. She went through the motions of being furious at them for taking her away from her support system, the gang, but in reality, she just didn't care anymore. She felt her life had ended back in Medellin when she killed her friend, and she was resigned to the stone-cold loneliness of existence with no heart and no hope.

Then she received the *Book of Hope* in her classroom in Quibdo. She might not have read it, because she didn't care about it or anything else. But the teacher got so excited about the book that she began to use it as the curriculum for the school's personal development course, so Leide was forced to read it. At first, it didn't mean anything more to her than her science book or civics book. Then slowly, it began to speak to her heart, a heart that had seemed encased in rock, or in ice. Somehow these words began to fight their way through the hard shell around Leide's heart.

When the opportunity came to attend a Book of Hope summer camp sponsored by the local church, Leide decided to go. There, she heard once again the story she had read in the book: the story of a Man who never sinned, and yet who was horribly punished for all the sins of the world! The story of a man who was sacrificed in place of Barabbas, a known murderer. Why, why had a Man so clean, pure and perfect allowed Himself to be tortured to death? Leide realized that Jesus had given His life in her place!

He had died for her sins … for every theft, every violent crime, every sexual sin, and even for the murder she had done back in Medellin. He could forgive her, and help to raise her to new life. Leide felt the possibility of hope and future begin to swell inside her, and felt those parts of her that had died that horrible day in Medellin begin to be reborn. She asked Jesus to forgive her for all her sins, and she pledged to live her life for Him.

The words of God in Ezekiel 36:26 came alive in her: "I will give you a new heart and put a new spirit in you; I will remove from you your heart of stone and give you a heart of flesh" (NIV).

Today at age 17, Leide is a vibrant young believer who is growing in God and in fellowship with her local church. She still struggles with regret over the horrible sins of her past, but God is at work in her. She has been reunited in a loving relationship with her family, is working hard on her studies at school, and has completely renounced her old, immoral lifestyle. Time turned a corner for Leide, and led her into new life with Jesus!

It took a few years for us to be invited into the schools of Nicaragua, but I met with then-President Daniel Ortega, and eventually we went to work with the national church to tell the children about Jesus. Some American teams went to help out, and the response in Nicaragua was wonderful. I heard about a little 12-year-old girl whose life was literally saved because of the *Book of Hope*. Maria had done the best she could to care for her three little brothers after their parents abandoned them. She quit school, and each morning at 3 a.m. she would awaken and begin preparing tortillas, which she would sell on the street later. In her "spare" time, Maria got her brothers up, fed them what little food they had, and sent them to school.

But she knew she couldn't keep it up. She was hungry and tired all the time, and it seemed to her that she had nothing to live for. Sadly, a lot of people in Maria's neighborhood felt the same way — and there was a popular new and quick way to commit suicide, by means of a chemical that was readily available. She knew that she would go to hell for committing suicide, but she didn't want her little brothers to feel abandoned, and perhaps commit suicide, and wind up in hell themselves. So Maria made the difficult choice that she would give her three brothers this suicide chemical before she took hers. At least, she reasoned, they would go to heaven.

This little family did not know Jesus. Their parents had left them with the vague notion that they had to be good to go to heaven, and she believed her brothers were good. The day Maria chose to carry out her plan, her little brothers came home with the *Book of Hope*. "Sister, read this book to us!" they called. She sat down with them and read of the wondrous love of Jesus. Right then and there, all four children committed their lives to Christ. They were even able to find the church that had provided the book, and there received help for their difficult circumstances.

It was a miracle for this young family. Their destiny was affected forever.

The nation of Cuba was a miracle for us. Despite the fall of the Soviet Union, this isolated island nation had remained staunchly Marxist, under the powerful hand of the powerful rule of Fidel Castro. Although we knew the national church was strong and growing, we were not able to send them anything because of barriers that stood between the government of Cuba and the rest of the world. It was such a delight then, to hear that Castro would allow a celebration of Protestantism in Cuba, and that the churches had invited us to send the *Book of Hope* for the children of Cuba!

The celebration was a great event, but the books wound up impounded in customs until after the Protestant party was over. The national believers did not let this stop them. When they finally received the books, they organized to get God's Word to the children. School distribution is not allowed, so the church divides the region into districts, and a certain church leader will be responsible for going to every house with children in that district. They drop the book off personally, speak to the students and parents, and ask the children to be sure to read through the book and answer the study questions. Then they return a week or so later, grade the study questions, go over them with the children and family, and present the Gospel right there. Hundreds of children and their parents have responded.

This method of distribution has turned out to be very useful for evangelism to children and adults alike. And in one case, it was a lifesaver for a woman who had come to the end of her rope in one poor neighborhood of Cuba.

She felt there was nothing left to live for, so she poisoned herself and sat down to wait for death.

There was a knock at the door, and she went to answer. There were the members of a local church. They were visiting every house in the area, leaving a gift for the children in each household. She told them there were no children here, but they sensed something was wrong ...

"We can give you this book," they suggested, and invited themselves in. They told her about the *Book of Hope*, and they shared the good news that Jesus loved her and could save her. Suddenly, the light went on inside her! She said that she wanted to accept Christ as Savior, and they led her in prayer. But then she confessed what she had done — she had already poisoned herself in a suicide effort!

One of the church members immediately left to bring a doctor, who arrived just in time to save the woman's life! Now she lives as a testimony to Christ's power to save, physically and spiritually.

There are more and more stories like this from across Latin America, where the *Book of Hope* has impacted an entire generation, and continues to touch the lives of children, their families, and their schools and teachers.

A funny thing happened to me and Rob, my son and the ministry's executive director, in Peru. We were making our way along a fairly well-lighted downtown street in Lima, Peru, but the gang of boys on the corner made me pause. They were teenagers in tattered jeans, oversized sports jerseys and their ball caps on backward, an outfit that in today's universal youth code translates into "looking-for-trouble." Fairly sure the boys didn't speak English, as Rob and I hurried by, I muttered to him something like, "Well, take a look at this motley crew."

"Motley Crüe?" one of the boys called. Surprised, we turned around. Did they speak English? What would their reaction be to what I had said? The response wasn't what I had feared.

Rob speaks some Spanish, so he understood when the teenager said, "You know Motley Crüe?" He was talking about a band. He turned his baseball cap around to show us the logo of the heavy metal band called Motley Crüe. Rob and I stopped and began to talk with the boys about the music of Motley Crüe, the other music kids in America like, and the differences between life here and there. So there I was, an American senior citizen, caught up in a face-to-face with Peruvian teenagers, just because they thought I knew about their favorite band. Eventually the talk turned to what Rob and I were doing in their city, and we were able to tell the boys about Jesus.

In a way it boggles my mind that bridging the gap between the barriers of Lima, Peru where they live and middle-class America where I live, has become so easy. But in other ways, I find it perfectly understandable and acceptable. You see, the fullness of time has come.

Chapter
Six

Ancient Rome began as a pagan empire that subjugated the known world under the dominion of the false gods they worshipped. Surely the one true God could not be honored through the worship of idols, yet He allowed this paganism to spread and even subdue His chosen people. At the time when Christ appeared on the scene, Israel had been ground under Rome's heel. That was one reason that the Hebrew religious leaders refused to believe that Christ could be the Messiah. How could God send His Son to an Israel that was enslaved and oppressed? That was also the reason Jesus' disciples had such a difficult time understanding that as Messiah, Jesus' program was not to overthrow the Roman overlords.

Why would God send the Savior at such a seemingly inopportune moment? Because that exact moment in history was the fullness of time for our salvation. The Romans thought they were subjugating the world to bring glory to their emperor. God knew pagans were subjugating the world so that His children could use the channels they established to carry the good news of Jesus Christ to the known world! The safe sea-lanes that Roman ships patrolled and the roads they built and monitored would soon allow Paul to take the Gospel to Rome, Thomas to carry the good news to India, and Andres deep into Central Asia. With the world united under one empire, First Century Christians were able to carry the message of salvation to the ends of the known world.

Yes, the same power that made it safe for them to become missionaries throughout the empire also persecuted and imprisoned them, even executing them in the arena ... but at the same time, the Word was carried everywhere, and believers were added to the church in a great explosion after Pentecost. The pagan empire of Rome facilitated the spread of the Gospel in a way that would have been impossible had Christ appeared on the scene earlier ... and eventually the power of the Gospel transformed the paganism of Rome.

Fast-forward 2000 years. I believe the fullness of time has arrived again, in our day. There has been an explosion in communication, information and technology. The devil has had his hand in it and had control of a lot of it. Look at the misery he has engendered through the worldwide web: Internet pornography sites are among the most visited, and one of the biggest selling products in web marketing is digital porn. Satan uses the Internet to make pornography available to anyone with a web connection. No more does the poor soul enslaved to lust and evil have to brave a visit to the adult bookstore or theater, or have the offensive materials delivered to his home for all to see. Now he can access it in secret on the web, pay with a credit card, and no one is the wiser. Think of the families that have been destroyed by this secrecy and sin. Then there is the lowest form of pornography, child pornography. In this case, it is not the porn addict I feel sorry for, but the children whose lives have been ruined when they were forced into these degrading acts and their innocence sold. It is disgusting.

The Internet also gave instant communications to dissatisfied spouses to shop secretly for a new mate while still married to the old one. They could meet the man or woman of their dreams in a chat room, converse online, even fall in love over the worldwide web. Countless divorces, broken homes and shattered families have begun that way. Sadly, the same technology can put sexual predators in contact with their next victims. Young girls looking for the love they feel is missing in their home and family life can connect with someone they think is another lonely teenager in a chat room. They agree to meet their new friend and find instead that he is an adult rapist or murderer.

Even in less extreme cases, the Internet can still be an enemy to families, as it takes up more and more of Mom or Dad's time with its endless array of amusements, games, shopping, chats, quizzes and other such drivel. Although it's a brilliant technology that would seem to make life easier, it has in fact made life much harder for some.

Likewise the latest movie and video technology, especially the photo-realistic animations that drive games like those for Nintendo, GameBoy, X-Box, Game Cube and so forth. While some of these games are just pure fun for kids, others desensitize youngsters to violence and numb their still growing brains. I believe there is no doubt that these games have a powerful impact on the habitual players. Just think about this:

Years ago, the U.S. military discovered that most young men have an aversion to killing anyone, and this was so even in wartime. Boys who could shoot and bayonet a target very accurately and quickly were failing to live up to their training in battle. They were just repulsed by the idea of killing actual human beings. What helped them overcome their revulsion and be better killers in actual combat was simply this: they trained using dummy humans instead of targets and hay bales. When their targets had human characteristics, and they could get used to shooting or bayoneting something that looked like the enemy they would face on the battlefield, they were much more likely to complete successful kills.

What are we doing to teenagers, whose minds are still developing, when we set realistic-looking human beings in front of them and encourage them to kill? Many popular video games are little more than that: a human-looking target to demolish. I wonder how many teenagers who murder have had honed their killing skills throughout their adolescence by playing video games?

It is wonderful technology, nothing short of what primitive people would consider magic. When Satan uses it to train kids for killing, it retains its power and can warp their minds. Television, too, is a great technology, but there are studies that show TV has actually helped to "dumb down" our society, because it has trained children to expect a constantly-changing variety of entertainment. If whatever they are currently engaged in doesn't live up to that standard, they want to be able to click away and start on something else. Studies have shown that the attention spans of today's children have actually shortened significantly from that of the last generation, attributable almost entirely to television and its endless flicker and flash. Another great technology, but it is being used to tear people down instead of to build them up.

Are the Internet, photo-realistic animation, TV, CD, and DVD actually the Roman Empire of our day? They have been conceived and used by pagans for destructive purposes, but they have also shrunk the world to the point that we can reach it with our message, via the same means. We just have to understand our times.

Thanks to TV and the Internet, the culture of American and European youth has become the global youth culture. That's why those boys in Lima could understand me when I called them a motley crew, even though they weren't thinking of the same "crew" that I was. Cell phones, satellites, movies and the worldwide web have demolished cultural barriers and united young people in their fashion, trends, speech, desires, and behaviors. It is possible today to speak to a larger segment of the worldwide population by means of a movie than ever before in history. If you have any doubt of that, just keep this in mind: more children and youth around the world are able to identify Arnold Schwarzenegger's character of "The Terminator" than can tell you who Jesus is.

My son Rob grew up on the mission field, so when he read of Christ's command to go to the "ends of the earth," his idea of the ends of the earth was way out there — Mongolia. For a boy who grew up between Lebanon, France and the USA, the most far off and exotic corner of the globe he could imagine was Mongolia. His daydreams about the mission field of Mongolia included people with blunt Asian features, draped in home-skinned and tanned ox leathers, imposing physiques and an incomprehensible language. Although God never called him to preach or serve in Mongolia, the place remained in his dreams as the literal ends of the earth.

So when he was on a plane in the former Soviet Union in the early days of this ministry, and they announced an unexpected stopover to take on passengers in Mongolia, Rob was thrilled. Now he was finally going to be in the land of his missions dreams and meet the Mongolians he had long imagined to be the last unreached people. What a crushing disappointment when the flight attendant told him that because of his U.S. Passport, he was not allowed off the plane. Undaunted, Rob decided he would at least get to meet some Mongolian people, for the plane had stopped to take on passengers, and the flight attendant told him some young Mongolian men and women bound for university in Moscow would be boarding. Rob sat on the plane while the Russian passengers were allowed to disembark and stretch their legs, and he anxiously watched for the arrival of the Mongolians.

They could hardly have been less like what he imagined. These young men and women were clad in blue jeans and t-shirts featuring logos and photos of the same rock bands that kids in the USA listen to. They had earphones to the Walkman radios on their belt clips, and some of them even spoke English. When Rob got a chance to have a conversation with them, he found them well informed on the popular musicians, athletes and movie stars of that moment — Madonna, Bruce Springsteen, Clint Eastwood, Michael Jordan. These were not the remote descendants of Genghis Khan that he had imagined the Mongolians to be. They were just like any of the university students in the U.S., Europe or Japan.

The world youth culture, international media and developing technology have united the next generation in the way they experience the world. Children in New York City play the same video games, watch the same MTV music videos and rent the same DVDs as youngsters in Johannesburg, South Africa and Paris, France. Because of this homogenous culture and available technology, it is easier now than ever before in history to reach huge segments of the international population with the good news. Globalization has created a fullness of time for us.

Like the technology that facilitated this change, perhaps the devil intended it for evil, or perhaps it was just a by-product of all the evil he has accomplished using the Internet, TV, movies and video games. But we don't have to let him use these things for evil any more, and by God's hand today, we can use them for good. In the book of Genesis, the mean-spirited brothers of Joseph threw him down a well, then sold him into slavery in Egypt. When he was elevated to second in command of the entire Egyptian kingdom, and they were starving in Palestine, they were horrified to think that he might remember their cruelty and repay them in kind.

But Joseph said, "Don't be afraid. Am I in the place of God? You intended to harm me, but God intended it for good to accomplish what is now being done, the saving of many lives" (Genesis 50:19,20, NIV).

What the devil intended for evil, God intended for good. What the devil has up until now used for evil, we may now use for good by God's power. The key is simply in understanding our times. The shrinking world has given us the most effective platform to preach our message of hope to the most children and youth in the least amount of time. And the powerful graphic technology that has driven mind-warping video games can now be used to present the timeless message of Jesus in a way that can embrace kids around the world. This is our moment to shine, and as we come together in unity of spirit, prayer and cooperation, we can reflect the light of Christ in a way that draws children and youth from around the world.

Jesus would not have asked us to preach the Gospel to every creature if there were no way to do it. Just as God allowed the Roman Empire to flourish despite its pagan origins, He now allows the communication, information and graphics technology to flourish, and it will carry our message of His love to an ever-shrinking world.

Chapter
Seven

When a pastors' conference in India invited me to speak to them about the *Book of Hope* in 1999, I was thrilled. This could be the break we had been waiting for, to begin giving God's Word to the children of India! When I had explained our program, the Indian pastors were enthusiastic. They immediately discounted the idea of going into the schools and working with students — they believed the government would never allow it — but they desperately wanted literature they could give to people through the churches. Could we send them the *Book of Hope* for that?

I had to refer back to the mission statement of the Book of Hope ministry: *to affect destiny around the world by providing God's eternal Word to all the children and youth of the world.* As much as I would have loved to give the *Book of Hope* to the churches of India for them to use in their church services and adult evangelism, that was not what God had called me to do. I explained the ministry and asked them to try to get permission to go into the schools, because as soon as they could, we would be back ... I didn't really see any way it could happen and left the conference a little discouraged.

The next day, a missionary arrived at the conference with

wonderful news! Her old boss had come to hear her preach the night before, and he had given his life to Christ. He happened to be the head of several schools in their area, and he wanted to know if there was some way he could get the Word of God into the hands of hundreds of thousands of Indian students! We began delivering God's Word to the children in those schools, and doors continued to open. Already we have given the *Book of Hope* to nearly 35 million students in India. Of course, there are still some 300 million to go, so we have our work cut out for us there. Please pray.

God is using the *Book of Hope* in remarkable ways in India. I think of a little nine-year-old girl named Sunni, who received the *Book of Hope* at school and committed her life to Christ. In her village, there was no church, and of course she and her family were all Hindus. But one day at the marketplace, Sunni saw the pastor from the neighboring village who had brought the *Book of Hope* to her school. She introduced him to her father, and her father invited the pastor home. The pastor explained the plan of salvation to the entire family, and each one chose to follow Jesus. Soon Sunni's dad began holding a Bible study in his home, and there are now 20 families faithfully living for Jesus and attending that Bible study.

Sujita was a 15-year-old Indian girl who also received the *Book of Hope* at school. This was a girl with troubles. Her father had been an alcoholic for most of his adult life, and now the booze was finally killing him. Sujita and her mother were going to be on their own with other children to provide for. When Sujita heard that this Scripture book had hope for her and her family, she listened intently to the pastor who was presenting it. And when he invited the students to make a commitment to Jesus right there at school, Sujita was one of the first ones to raise her hand. She joyfully committed her life to Christ.

Then she went home, sat down with her mother, brothers and sisters, and explained Jesus to them. She showed them the book, told them the story, and also shared that she had decided to follow Jesus. They all agreed with her decision, and they all decided to follow Jesus, too! Plus, they began to pray for their father's salvation and healing. Within two months of the day Sujita brought the *Book of Hope* home, her father also made a commitment to Christ, and his physical health was restored. Today, Sujita's family is growing in Christ and active in their local church.

Birsingh's family was in sort of the same situation as Sujita's. They lived in a poor neighborhood in western India. Not everyone could read and write, but many of the youngsters were attending school and learning what their parents never learned. Birsingh's son was one of those lucky boys, and he received the *Book of Hope* at school.

He brought it home and began to read it, and that's when Birsingh noticed it. "What have you got there?" he demanded. "What are you so interested in?" Birsingh was an alcoholic, and he terrorized his wife and three children on an almost daily basis. His little boy was terrified by his father's sudden interest in his new book.

Timidly, he began, "This is a book I got from school. It is about a good man named Jesus ..." Birsingh didn't explode immediately, so the boy went on telling him what he had read about Jesus. It intrigued Birsingh, but it also confused him, especially when his son read to him how Christ died for our sins. If Jesus was a perfect holy man, why would he die for Birsingh's sins?

Some members of the local church came to visit Birsingh's children to find out if they had read the *Book of Hope* yet. Were they ever surprised to find the belligerent Birsingh inviting them into the house and asking them question after question about Jesus! That day, Birsingh, his wife, and their three youngsters all made a commitment to live for Jesus. They now attend the local church, and their lives have been transformed by God's love!

This is the power of God's Word to affect destiny, even in nations where people sometimes say it is impossible to win souls to Jesus. But in India, the *Book of Hope* has not only won entire families to the faith, it has also become a wonderful tool for planting new churches. Witness the story of Jony and his dad:

Jony was a nine-year-old boy. His father, Dheeraj, suffered from crippling arthritis, and he had been bed-ridden for more than a year. There was so little hope or happiness in their home in India's West Bengal ... Then Jony received the *Book of Hope* in his school. He was so excited to read in its pages about a man who could make the lame walk and the blind see that he hurried home with the book for his father.

Dheeraj, too, was intrigued, and the following Sunday the whole family helped him get out of bed and slowly make their way to the local church, to find out more about Jesus. There, the entire family decided to follow Jesus. Then everyone prayed for Dheeraj, and for the first time he was able to stand without help!

Today, there is new happiness in Jony's home. His father now distributes the same book that first told him about Jesus, and he pastors one of the 28 churches planted in West Bengal using the *Book of Hope*.

The *Book of Hope* turned Jony into a missionary to his father, and then God's call turned Dheeraj into a pastor who gives the *Book of Hope* to other children like Jony and ministers to other families like his own. What power there is in the Word of God!

This is God's moment for children and youth in India, across the rest of Asia, and around the world. The only real question is if we as believers are ready to step up and seize our moment. The Bible encourages us, "Teach us to number our days aright, that we may gain a heart of wisdom" (Psalm 90:12, NIV). Time, as it turns out, is our only important commodity, for without it, the rest of our abilities and resources are meaningless. One young woman who had to learn very quickly to number her days and use her time wisely is Queen Esther in the Old Testament.

You may know her story well: one of those gems of the Bible, a love story that combines excitement, suspense, near disaster and miraculous rescue — all upon the slim shoulders of a lovely Hebrew heroine.

The powerful King Xerxes ruled over the Persian Empire, and had arranged a beauty contest for the loveliest women from across his huge kingdom, searching for a new queen. Young Esther was entered in the contest by her uncle Mordecai, a palace official who had raised her as a daughter after her parents died. I don't know how Esther felt about all this because the Bible doesn't tell us. Perhaps it's an indication that when our duty to God becomes clear, how we feel about doing it doesn't really enter into the equation.

However, maybe Esther didn't mind the first part of the challenge: she was taken to the palace, assigned seven maids to care for her, given the best of food and a regimen of beauty treatments for a whole year. After all this, she was presented to the king, who loved her and chose her as his new queen. Now as Esther began her new life as Queen of Persia, she was oblivious to the fact that Mordecai had made an enemy at the palace, an evil man named Haman — and that Haman was plotting to kill him and all the Jews in Persia. By the time Esther's uncle could get this news to her, a huge public gallows had already been constructed to hang her Uncle Mordecai! The disaster was almost upon them.

Mordecai begged Esther to go to the king and plead their case, but she was stalled by a law that prevented anyone, even the queen, from going into the king's presence without an invitation. She could be killed for breaking that law! Nevertheless, Mordecai urged her to take her chances. In one of the most powerful Scriptures in all of the Bible, he told her:

"… if you remain silent at this time, relief and deliverance for the Jews will arise from another place, but you and your father's family will perish. And who knows but that you have come to royal position for such a time as this?" (Esther 4:14, NIV).

Trust God with your life, Mordecai says. Abandon yourself to His will at this time, because it is your time.

I believe there are many parallels between the life of Esther and the American church today. And I believe this is our time — that like Esther, we have been raised for such a time as this. Let's compare ourselves to her:

> 1. We live with unprecedented wealth. Like Esther, the church in America has more material wealth and resources than ever before. There is not a country or a culture that has ever had more money, luxury and things. But like Esther, we also need to understand why we have been entrusted with so much.

> 2. We have been oblivious to the danger around us. It's easy to make the comparison between Haman's evil forces at work in the Persian Empire and the radical Islamic forces that attacked America on September 11, 2001 and plunged us into the war on terrorism. But I think we, as the church in America, have been oblivious to an even more real danger: the erosion of faith in our nation and what it has done to the next generation.

Not long ago, my son Rob showed me an incredible article in *Atlantic Monthly* entitled, "The Apocalypse of Adolescence." It outlined in chilling detail a burst of teen violence in, of all places, the state of Vermont. Most of us think of peaceful Vermont as a gorgeous New England vacation spot for those crisp autumn days when the leaves begin to turn and God puts on a spectacular show of color and natural grace. Were we to imagine growing up in the state of Vermont, maybe we would envision small-town closeness and idyllic days of bike-riding, church-going, and harmony. The outward look of peace and tranquility we associate with Vermont has not changed, but the shocking actions of Vermont's teenagers defies it.

The article documented a five-year period in small-town Vermont (centered on the suburban town of Chelsea) where five people were murdered by teenagers and another was brutally assaulted. Seven kids were arrested in connection with the murders, and two for the assault. The state itself has one of the lowest crime rates in the union, yet the article reported that the number of jail inmates aged 16-21 had increased by over 77% in three years. The high school dropout rate had increased by almost 50%, and heroin abuse had become "an established crisis" with underage addicts in virtually every town of substantial size in Vermont.

The same week that *Atlantic Monthly* released this strange and sad article, the *USA Today* newspaper had a report on faith and belief in God across the USA. It appeared that more and more people were becoming atheists or agnostics. Washington ranked as the number one most agnostic state, and right behind it in position number two was the state of Vermont. Although the secular authorities refuse to see any connection between loss of faith and teen violence, the parallel to me is obvious and glaring.

The state of Vermont still looks idyllic, and its pastoral settings and lovely landscapes, combined with its low crime rate and sterling reputation, deceive us into thinking that it is indeed as close to a paradise as can be found in the USA. Families move there with the hopes that their children will grow up healthy, connected and whole. But Vermont is also a state where many people don't believe in God, thus they don't teach their children about God, and among the next generation a moral root rot is setting in.

There are other dangers just as dramatic in other countries, and we seem just as oblivious to them. The genocide of AIDS taking place in South Africa is set to outpace the Holocaust by millions. We don't see it happening, so we are oblivious to it. We don't seem to understand that Jesus meant what He said when He told us the thief comes to steal, kill and *destroy*. There is danger to the next generation all around us.

Children have been forced to become soldiers in many nations of Asia and Africa, and children have also been forced to become prostitutes. In nations such as India, Thailand and Cambodia, little girls — and many little boys as well — have been kidnapped or sold into sexual slavery. Perverts from around the world routinely come to these countries for pedophile-themed vacations, where they can buy sex with children as young as six or eight years old. In Cambodia and Thailand, these poor children are known as "the dead girls," because statistics show that within seven years of their arrival at the brothel, they will be dead. Since 1990, 30 million children around the world have been sold into sexual exploitation and abuse. These are babies, little children, their childhood crushed, their innocence stolen.

Such dangers threaten millions of children and youth around the world today, and sad to say, we are almost totally unaware of it … like Esther in her palace. Haman was a snake in the grass, her husband's close advisor, right there in the palace with her, and she never sensed his evil until her uncle confronted her with it.

Rob was recently preaching in rural Oklahoma. As he drove though the lush farmland and observed the white picket fences, he said he felt he was driving back into time, into a Norman Rockwell painting. As he pulled up to the pristine country church and saw the wholesome families filing in together, he thought of the horrible condition of children he has met around the world — child prostitutes in Cambodia, AIDS victims in Africa, teenage drugs addicts in Russia — and he thought how wonderful it would be if all of them could be rescued and brought to a safe, serene environment like the one surrounding the children and youth of rural Oklahoma.

At the end of his message to the church that night, the pastor of this rural congregation in the middle of the "Bible Belt" spoke to Rob, hesitantly asking, "Will you please pray for my son? He has been arrested for dealing drugs." A moment later, an elderly farmer stepped up and said, "Please pray for my grandson. He spoke to me yesterday, and he is so confused. He thinks he is a homosexual." You see, no one is safe, no matter how serene and secure the circumstances may look to the human eye. Satan is using every weapon in his arsenal against the next generation, at home and abroad.

So there is a third lesson we can learn from Esther's story:

3. We must abandon ourselves to God's keeping or abandon God. Esther was forced suddenly into the biggest decision of her life — whether to risk death by going into the presence of the king unbidden, or to desert

her faith and her family by letting them die at Haman's hands. This, too, parallels the situation we, as believers in America, find ourselves in today.

There was never a time when we were excused from observing and understanding the dangers around us, nor from responding to them as we were able, but in the past, we could not respond to all of them. Today, the church has been endowed with such abundant resources and given such powerful tools that there is no excuse for our continued inaction or apathy. We may not be able to cure AIDS, and we may not be able to stop wars, and we may not have a psychological degree or a criminal justice background to bring violent teenagers back into line.

What we do have is an instantaneous communications network, a vast force of Christ-followers, the Word of God in a variety of languages and formats, and — if we abandon ourselves to it — the power of God inside us to share with every human being on earth! Never before has any generation had all this at its disposal, and God help us if we refuse to abandon ourselves to Him and allow Him to take us where He will by the means of these resources and tools.

Yes, there's a chance we may die, but don't you think God is looking for people willing to take that chance? Esther knew there was the very real chance that she would be executed for her daring move of going into the king's presence without his invitation. It was the law! But this was her moment. This was her time. Her message to her uncle was this: Pray for me, and I will do it. "I will go to the king, even though it is against the law. And if I perish, I perish" (Esther 4:16, NIV).

I believe this is the attitude Jesus is looking for today among His followers: the attitude of a people who have weighed what their lives are worth, who have measured their days, and who have realized that long life at the expense of their faith and relationship with God is not worth having. Choose today whether you will abandon yourself to God, or abandon Him.

4. We have the potential for the biggest comeback story

in history. Esther's overwhelming victory against evil is one of the Bible's greatest turnarounds. The king does not order her killed, but he willingly calls her to his side and offers to grant her any wish. By his hand, she is able to save her people. The treacherous Haman ends up swinging on the rope from the gallows he intended for Mordecai. And Mordecai himself is exalted as a hero.

Likewise, the church today can yet see their great turnaround, their great comeback story, too. It depends on our ability to understand why God has given us the resources He has given us, to recognize the danger around us, and finally to willingly abandon ourselves to His plan for us and confidently echo Esther's heart-felt words, "If I perish, I perish."

God is looking for a generation that will abandon everything to Him and understand that they have been born for such a time as this. Just as Esther overcame Haman, we, too, can overcome the enemy who is devastating the next generation. The turnaround story of world missions in our lifetime can still be told, by you and by me. We can be the generation that finally fulfills the Great Commission and brings the Savior back for His saints, if we follow in Esther's footsteps.

Mark 16:15 was not a suggestion or an option. It was a mandate that Christ placed upon His church and expected us to fulfill.

Chapter Eight

In the African nation of Burkina Faso, 10-year-old Miriam was desperate. She and her mother had watched her father slowly die from AIDS, and then just a few months later, Miriam's mother began to show symptoms of the disease. Because of the stigma of AIDS in Africa, victims are shunned and ostracized. Miriam's grandparents and aunts and uncles came and forced Miriam and her mother to leave their village!

Miriam knew what would happen. She had seen AIDS waste away and kill her father — but at least then, her mother had been there to care for him. Soon her mother would need constant care — and who would be there to provide it except Miriam, alone, a 10-year-old child?

Miriam's mother was not a believer, but thank God, sometime in her own childhood she had attended classes at a missionary school. Although she was miserably ill, she managed to get herself and her daughter to the nearest village and look for a Christian church. Perhaps they could help her.

Against all odds, it turned out that the local pastor and his congregation were able to help. The pastor had attended an AIDS-training seminar in response to the terrible disease that is ravaging the African continent, and he mobilized his church. They found a family to take in Miriam and her mother, and they even managed to come up with the funds for some low-cost healthcare. Miriam's mom still has HIV, but the AIDS symptoms have tapered off, and both Miriam and her mother have given their hearts to Jesus.

What a wonderful story of God's people reaching out to those in need! I wish it could happen for every little girl like Miriam and every struggling mom, but the problem in Africa looks so overwhelming:

- In 2001, there were 12.1 million AIDS orphans in sub-Saharan Africa. It's now predicted that by decade's end, 40 million children will have lost their parents to AIDS.
- Sub-Saharan Africa accounts for 70% of the total world-wide population of people living with HIV/AIDS and 80% of the children living with HIV in the world.
- 3/4 of the world's AIDS deaths have taken place in Africa.

In South Africa alone:

- A conservative estimate says that 1/3 of all deaths are because of AIDS.
- About 20% of the population is infected nationally, and in KwaZulu-Natal, the hardest hit area of South Africa, 35% are HIV positive.
- That accounts for 500 AIDS deaths a day in KwaZulu-Natal and by 2005, it is estimated that there will be 16,000 AIDS deaths every single day in South Africa.

Children are the largest people group on the African continent. Nearly 50% are age 15 or under. I believe there is still time to reach these kids with the hope of Jesus, and that is the reason I try so hard to get our children's Scripture book, the *Book of Hope*, into the hands of children and youth in Africa.

My wife Hazel and I had our first home as a married couple when we were missionaries in Africa, a mud hut with a cow-dung floor. But we were as happy as we could be there, because of the wonderful warmth of the African people and the fulfillment of doing the work to which God had called us. Hazel and I loved our time in Africa, and the people of those nations still hold a special place in our hearts. That's one reason, as the *Book of Hope* ministry began to spread from Latin America to Europe and Asia, that we longed to be able to take God's Word to the children of Africa.

When that door finally seemed to be opening, we went to Africa to coordinate the ministry with the national church, and what we saw in Africa was so deeply moving ... I watched a presentation of the *Book of Hope* to a high school assembly with over 1,600 students. These beautiful kids looked healthy to me. But when the team asked anyone infected with HIV to come forward for prayer, more than half the students came forward, already HIV-positive. It broke my heart.

And it is not just the AIDS virus. The various nations on the continent of Africa have suffered from war, poverty and violence, and the children are the victims. In many warring nations of Africa (and around the world), children are actually abducted and placed on the battlefronts as soldiers.

- In Uganda, 10,000 children have been kidnapped and forced into the ranks.
- Newsweek reports that "soldiers" under age 15 have fought in half of the world's 55 ongoing or just-ended wars.
- Afghanistan, Eritrea, Ethiopia, Somalia and several other nations accept or conscript boys under age 18 into the government armies.

Listen to these words from a May 13, 2002 *Newsweek* article, spoken by an African boy named Alieu, who was nine years old when he was abducted and forced to go to war:

"Six rebels came through our yard ... They said, 'We want to bring a small boy like you — we like you.' My mother didn't comment; she just cried. My father objected. They threatened to kill him. They argued with him at the back of the house. I heard a gunshot. One of them told me, 'Let's go.

They've killed your father.' A woman rebel grabbed my hand roughly and took me along. I saw my father lying dead as we passed."

This horror may not even be the worst of it, for Alieu was then given drugs and taught to fight. He killed not only in battle, but mercilessly mutilated and murdered prisoners of war and refugees, all before age 14.

The precious boys and girls of Africa desperately need help, and hope. Thank God, we have begun reaching the children of Africa with the *Book of Hope*. I think of our alliance with the Teen Challenge ministry in South Africa. Teen Challenge is a great faith-based rehab program that has one of the best, if not *the* best, success rate in helping victims of life-controlling addiction overcome their problems.

In South Africa, there is a great move toward getting drug prevention efforts in the schools, and we have teamed up with Teen Challenge in South Africa to take God's Word to the students. One of the stories that stands out most vividly to me is that of a Teen Challenge graduate who suffered sexual abuse as a child, and was driven into drug addiction in her hopeless attempts to escape from the pain of the past. When she gave her life to Christ and came into the Teen Challenge program, she found the strength she needed to defeat addiction, and she also found healing for the open wounds of her past.

She went into one of the schools with the Affect Destiny Team in South Africa, and there the teacher told her that many of the little girls in the classroom had been sexually abused. Because of the evil lies of Satan passed through the tribal witch doctors, AIDS victims believe that having sex with a virgin will cure them. So these depraved adult men try to insure they have found a virgin by raping young girls just four or five, or even two or three years old. It doesn't cure their AIDS, and it ruins the lives of these precious babies. At school, the mother of one of these poor little girls was weeping as she spoke to the team, "How can we heal them? How can we even connect with them?" she asked.

Then this young team member stood in front of the class, and from the horrible store of her own memories and experiences, she told these little girls her own tale of heartbreak and abuse. She shared with them that she understood their pain because she had not only been through it, but even went beyond it. She had tried to escape the pain through drugs, and that only brought about more pain. But there was a way to healing, and she had found it, and she could share it with them. "If you have experienced sexual abuse, and you want healing for the pain you still feel, come forward," she said.

Many of the young girls came forward. Some just collapsed into her arms in tears. When they heard her story, it came from a place they understood, an experience they'd been through themselves, and it touched their hearts in ways other words never could.

God's Word brings hope and healing, even in the bleakest night of hopelessness. It worked for a young lady named Pinkie in South Africa. She had moved from her hometown to the big city of Johannesburg. When she found herself alone and penniless, a friend told her to get a boyfriend who would pay her way. Soon Pinkie was moving from one boyfriend to another. The men paid her or bought her things for as long as she slept with them. Finally, she scraped up the money to get a ticket home, to her parents and family.

When she arrived there, everything changed for Pinkie. There was *Book of Hope* distribution in the schools, and Hope Fest crusades at night. The dynamic Gospel music of the group Knowdaverbs attracted Pinkie to the crusades, and there she met Jesus!

Today at age 23, Pinkie is a strong believer, and she recently completed training with our Book of Hope Response Teams to present music, drama and the *Book of Hope* to more kids in the schools of South Africa.

Then there is Enine. She is a beautiful 15-year-old South African girl, whose family struggled with abject poverty. Most of the time, there was enough to eat, but just barely. And Enine didn't live in any dusty slum. She lived in a regular city, Heilbron, where she had been exposed to all the stuff that's important for 15-year-olds to know in this day and age. Kids grow up pretty fast in South Africa these days, and Enine wanted desperately to be grown up, especially if it meant she could have some clothes and jewelry of her own.

That's why when the nice people from the Church of Satan offered to give her clothes and jewelry, she was overwhelmed! Clothes and jewelry were exactly what she wanted! And as for the church of Satan, well, it didn't sound that great, but at least they gave her presents. Enine decided to join. Wouldn't her friends be impressed when they saw all her new things?!

Enine's circumstances represent those of millions of children and youth around the world who are being courted by cults and false faiths today. It's not just the Church of Satan. It's the Mormons, the Moonies, the various New Age factions, as well as Hare Krishna, Hinduism, Islam and Buddhism. The ones who happened to reach out to Enine were from the Church of Satan, and she fell hard for them. She started sneaking out at night to attend midnight black masses. When she was supposed to baby-sit with her younger brother and sister, they threatened to tell their mother that she was leaving them alone, and she beat them until they promised not to tell!

Then Enine received the *Book of Hope* at school, and started reading about Jesus. Her first thought was that, as a Satanist, she should throw the book away, or burn it. But the more she read, the more intriguing the story became. When she read how Satan had tempted Jesus in the wilderness, she recognized herself in the story! Satan had tempted her with clothes and jewelry, and she had accepted.

Next she read about the little girl that Jesus raised from the dead, and that gave her a reason to hope. In South Africa, about one out of every five people is HIV-positive, and death is an oppressive reality, everywhere. Enine had been desperately afraid that she, too, might die, as so many girls her age and just a little older have. But in the pages of the *Book of Hope*, she found a man who could defeat death! Time turned a corner for Enine, and she joyfully gave her heart to Jesus. Then she returned the new clothes and jewelry to the church of Satan. Today, Enine, her mother and her little brother and sister have all come to Christ and attend church together.

Satan is waging war on kids around the world, but our prayers and God's Word can strike back against him and rescue the perishing.

I think the stories of Miriam, Enine, and Pinkie demonstrate how powerful God's Word is, and His love is, for the children of South Africa. The stories of Jony, Sujita and Sunni in India did the same — and the stories of Volodya, Irina, and Sasha in Russia, too. Why all these stories? Rob told me not long ago that a friend of his had called with an interesting insight as to why the *Book of Hope* works so well to win children and families to Jesus. It has to do with stories.

If you look at Mark chapter four in *The Message*, you'll see it clearly illustrated. *The Message* is Eugene H. Peterson's contemporary-language paraphrase of the Bible, and I will be using it for the next few Scripture references.

In Mark 4, Jesus tells the story, or parable, of the sower. Right away, this connects with His audience, because they are farmers or depend on farmers, and they understand the concepts of sowing and reaping. In the story, some seed fell on the road and birds ate it, some fell in the gravel and sprouted but never put down roots, some fell among weeds and were strangled by the weeds, and some fell on good ground and gave a great harvest. Then, the Bible says:

"When they were off by themselves, those who were close to Him, along with the Twelve, asked about the stories. He told them, 'You've been given insight into God's kingdom — you know how it works. But to those who can't see it yet, everything comes in stories, creating readiness, nudging them toward receptive insight.' ... He continued, 'Do you see how this story works? All my stories work this way.'"

Jesus knows that a good story gets people interested in what you have to say. I like the stories in Mark chapter four for a lot of reasons, but especially because each one has a happy ending. The parable of the sower ends up like this, "But the seed planted in the good earth represents those who hear the Word, embrace it, and produce a harvest beyond their wildest dreams." Now who would *not* want a harvest beyond their wildest dreams? And all we have to do in order to get it is to hear and embrace the Word!

Then Jesus tells a couple of shorter stories to illustrate the kingdom of God, and one of them is the most apropos for this book, "Does anyone bring a lamp home and put it under a washtub or beneath the bed? Don't you put it up on a table or on the mantel? We're not keeping secrets, we're telling them; we're not hiding things, we're bringing them out into the open."

Jesus is talking about the light, and showing us through the story how useless it is to receive the light inside us, and then hide it and never share it with a world in need! If we choose to be saved, and then never grow another inch in our relationship with Jesus, then we have failed to listen, really listen, to this story! If we accept Christ and then continue to accept the values of the secular, relativistic world, then we have not grasped the power of the light. Jesus goes on, "Listen carefully to what I am saying — and be wary of the shrewd advice that tells you how to get ahead in the world on your own. Giving, not getting, is the way. Generosity begets generosity. Stinginess impoverishes."

Here the Master is telling us something that flies in the face of what 21st Century logic dictates. The movies, TV, media — it all tells us to look out for number one, to get what we can while the getting is good. Jesus says all that is malarkey, and the way to life is through *giving*, not getting. I love that part.

But there's more. Jesus tells the story of a man who sows his seed, then goes to bed and forgets about it. The seed sprouts and grows up, and the farmer has no idea how that happens. He couldn't *make* it happen on command if he wanted to, but it happens in God's great design, naturally, and in its season. "The earth does it all without his help: first a green stem of grass, then a bud, then the ripened grain. When the grain is fully formed, he reaps — harvest time!"

Are you sensing a theme here? Every story Jesus tells has a happy ending, and in two cases now, the happy ending has been "harvest." Harvest is the joyful time when we bring in the rewards of all we have worked hard for. This is the beautiful ending of the story. Success, reward, harvest. Next, Jesus casts about for another illustration:

"How can we picture God's kingdom? What kind of story can we use? It's like a pine nut. When it lands on the ground it is quite small as seeds go, yet once it is planted it grows into a huge pine tree with thick branches. Eagles nest in it."

Once again, Jesus' story starts out with something small and insignificant, like a seed, and ends with something tall, strong, and beautiful, a great healthy tree so big that huge eagles can make their home in it. Another happy ending. The beautiful thing is that in each of these stories, Jesus is making an illustration for the kingdom of heaven. We also have the history of the kingdom of heaven in our Bible, to compare each story to, and each one is a perfect illustration. In one man, Adam, the human race began, and through one man, Adam, sin entered the world. That seed was planted long ago, and although we could do nothing to save ourselves from it, in the fullness of time God sent Jesus, our mighty strongman, to defeat sin and bring us into the fullness of life. We see the kingdom of heaven moving from a tiny seed to a great harvest, "a harvest beyond their wildest dreams."

Jesus is a great story-teller. His stories are wonderful. The Bible says, "With many stories like these, He presented His message to them, fitting the stories to their experience and maturity. He was never without a story when He spoke."

Did you ever consider that? Jesus never gave a sermon

without telling a story to illustrate His point. His message was communicated in pictures and comparisons to real-life events, experiences and things that His listeners were familiar with. The *Book of Hope* is presented to the children and youth of the world with just the same strategy! It is not a book of importuning to right living, but the living and active story of the life of Jesus Christ.

And we fit the story "to their experience and maturity," just as Jesus taught us to do. While each *Book of Hope* contains the Scripture text that tells the life story of Jesus in the age-specific language a child or youth can understand, we have also packaged the book in the most eye-appealing way and have added important sections to each book that concentrate on the issues most vital to the students at different age groups.

For instance, my son Rob's daughters are in the age group called "Tween." These are children approximately age 9-13. Educational specialists used to rank children as early elementary, elementary, junior high (or middle school) and then high school. But these days, we have been able to identify and more tightly focus on individual groups within those groupings, including the Tweens. What makes a Tween different from other elementary school age students, according to the latest research?

Tweens are so named because they are in the important stage *between* childhood and adolescence. What the research shows is that they differ from teenagers and younger children in several points, including:

> • They still have and value the moral compass instilled by their parents. As teens, the drive for independence will force them to reconsider their parent's morality and try to come up with their own moral gauge. (For teens who are already believers, this comes in the realization that they now honor God and His commands because of their own commitment to Christ, not because of the fact that the morality may have been handed down to them by mom and dad).

- They are just beginning to look outside the family for affirmation and a reflection of self. Little kids are still pretty much restricted to the family for influence/affirmation, and teenagers are actively trying to shrug off the family, but Tweens are just beginning to reach beyond the family. The media has latched onto this with intense advertising campaigns to these youngsters, especially the little girls, encouraging them to emulate popular musicians and TV and movie stars.

- They are still attached to parents, especially mom. As teenagers, they will sever that tie regarding thought and behavior and begin looking more to peers for behavioral cues. Tweens differ from younger children in that while they still have an attachment to mom, they are also at the stage where they begin to desire and experiment with their first taste of independence from the family (but also desire to be able to return to it).

As you read this short list, do you see what I see? This is the perfect developmental stage to introduce a desired behavioral change. Tweens still have that moral compass in place, but they are also beginning to look for new ways to define themselves. It is the perfect moment to introduce them to Jesus and show them how to define themselves through His love and plan. The whole key is simply to give them this message in a format they are drawn to and can understand. Just like Jesus, matching His story to His listeners' experience and maturity level.

We wanted to fit our message of hope to the "experience and maturity level" of the Tweens, just as Jesus fit His stories to the people He wanted to reach. So our Tween version of the *Book of Hope* looks like the most popular magazines for this group.

My granddaughters, who have seen so many *Books of Hope* in so many languages and formats that they don't even pay attention anymore, were impressed. "This is great! This is the best *Book of Hope* ever," they agreed. And it's not just the slick and modern look that makes this book special. We have also designed the extra issues sections to speak directly to the struggles that Tweens face and the questions they have. These are boys and girls about to embark on adolescence, and they have lots of questions. Yet they are still guided by the morality instilled in them by their parents and open to defining themselves in a way that is compatible with that ethical compass. The *Book of Hope* speaks a life-changing message directly to them.

We have specific versions of the *Book of Hope* for many different target age groups, and we have also created country-specific versions to better speak to the students in each country. This takes into account dialect and language differences, as well as the particular needs and issues in a specific country. We fit our book to the experience and maturity level of our readers.

And it is not just the book that we tailor to the audience, but the personal presentations of the book, too. We also encourage our local teams and volunteer teams from North America to tell stories of their own lives and experiences that will capture the imagination of the students they speak with.

Chapter
Nine

From our breakthrough opportunity to reach every child in the nation of El Salvador with God's Word in 1987, to our milestone of placing the *Book of Hope* into the hands of the 200 millionth child to receive it in 2003, God has wonderfully blessed the *Book of Hope* ministry and our efforts to reach every child with the printed Word of God, and we believe He will continue to do so.

But not long ago, we were confronted with a major roadblock to the ministry of the *Book of Hope*.

There's a saying in Latin, *Litera scripta manet,* which means, "The written word endures." Surely that has been true down through the ages, and at different stages in history, the power of the written word has been used in remarkable ways. I'm not talking just about the printed Word of God, but the printed word in general. You know who recognized the power of the printed word? The Marxists and communists. Books, pamphlets, flyers and booklets were easily as powerful as sabers and bullets in sparking the Russian Revolution. And then, when communism was established in the Soviet Union, the printed word helped to export communism to Africa, Latin America and beyond.

When the *Book of Hope* became in demand for Russia, we began investigating how to print the books on-site in Russia, and we found this was one of the best-equipped nations in the world for publications. Why? Because for 70 years they had been developing and printing communist propaganda that went around the world. People read. And when people in pain read about a way to ease their suffering, they remember, and they believe. That's how Marxism started to spring up in nations like Nicaragua and Peru. People read about it, and then embraced it.

Mein Kampf touched the hearts of people in post World War I Germany. A *Communist Manifesto* touched the hearts of discontented Bolsheviks in the early 20th Century. Chairman Mao's Little Red Book of sayings won the hearts of the common people of China and touched off the Cultural Revolution.

There is power in the printed word, and we have seen that even in the United States. What touched off the so-called "sexual revolution" in the USA? Pornography — and not just the filthy "girlie" magazine, but rather the modern novel. Are there any chaste heroines or sexually pure protagonists in the books that defined the sexual revolution? *Scruples* was an international bestseller of that era, and it is a chronicle of irresponsible sexual behavior. And the new freedom that liberated sex from its foundation in love and marriage has done more to damage the family unit and basic morality than perhaps any other change in American lifestyles. Once again, the printed word exerts its power to change behavior … in this case, in a negative fashion.

But God and His people have learned to use the power of the printed page, too. We have seen immense response to the *Book of Hope* among the schoolchildren and literate youth who have received it. But here is the problem, exemplified in some little boys from Madagascar who received a bracelet from their friends in North America.

Many Book of Hope partners take part in the "Hand in Hand" program that uses Hope Bracelets, based on the concept of the Salvation Bracelet, with five colored beads that tell a story. The yellow bead represents the gold streets of heaven, the dark bead, sin in our life that keeps us from heaven, the red bead, the blood of Jesus, the white bead, our souls that have been cleansed, and the green bead, the way we grow in God. We provide the leather bracelet and beads, and you assemble bracelets and save money in Book of Hope banks. These banks hold $5 in quarters, so when full, each bank will provide the *Book of Hope* for 15 children. You return 15 bracelets with each full Book of Hope Bank, and we deliver the books and the bracelets to the children, with your love.

Sunday school classes love putting these bracelets together to send as gifts to children around the world, and we have found that seniors, too, love this ministry. Although they may not be able to go on an Affect Destiny Team mission, they can certainly send $5 to give the *Book of Hope* to 15 children and make 15 bracelets. It's a wonderful way to be part of the movement, part of fulfilling the Great Commission in our lifetime.

It's an easy way to send the Gospel, plus a special gift of the bracelet, to the children of the world. And the bracelet is a very effective way to tell the story of salvation, too. A pastor in Madagascar was leaving school after a *Book of Hope* distribution. A little boy from school came up and asked if he could have the *Book of Hope* for some of his little friends who don't attend school. Unfortunately, the program is so regulated that there had been just enough books for all the students in the school — but the pastor did have extra Hope Bracelets. He gave one to the little boy, then explained to him what the bracelet meant, and even showed him a place in the *Book of Hope* where the same color illustrations are used to tell about Jesus. As he left the school, he saw that little boy, surrounded by his friends, using his bracelet and book to explain to them about Jesus!

Thank God this pastor was able to use the Hope Bracelet to share the Gospel, but the situation raised a real red flag. The sad fact is that even with the *Book of Hope* translated into dozens of languages for students around the world, it is no help at all to the 32% of children and youth around the world who cannot read. One of the other pastors in Madagascar brought up this very issue to us. He said, "Thank you so much for sending the *Book of Hope*. It is just what the children need, and the response has been wonderful! But most of the children here aren't in school and can't read. Is there anything you can do for them?"

That's a good question, especially when you consider the mission statement of the Book of Hope ministry: To affect the destiny of the next generation by providing God's Word to every child and youth in the world.

Okay, God, You gave us this mission, and now we have a whole huge segment of the population that cannot be reached with the printed *Book of Hope* because they cannot read it. Further study revealed that there are four distinct and populous groups of children and teenagers that by and large cannot be reached with the *Book of Hope*:

1. Illiterate

There are 690 million children and youth who cannot read, that is 32% of all youngsters around the world. These are boys and girls who may never be able to read in the foreseeable future simply because adequate schools are not available to them.

2. Preliterate

These are boys and girls who are four to seven years old, some 504 million kids worldwide. Although they may soon learn to read, right now we cannot reach them with the Gospel through the *Book of Hope*. Yet many children in this age bracket are capable of understanding the Gospel and are able to make a commitment to Christ.

Further, the younger we reach kids, the better opportunity we have to lead them to Christ. The statistics today show that most adult believers made their decision to live for Jesus at age 14 or earlier. The newest missions information says that there is a critical 4/14 Window, where we must reach children between the ages of 4 and 14 with the good news that Jesus loves them and motivate them to come to Christ. Yet some of the youngsters in this category, especially in Third World nations, can't read yet, and can't be reached with the *Book of Hope* — others in those same nations cannot be reached with the printed Word of God because they are in the third category:

3. Alliterate

A prime example of the "alliterate" is an American Tween or Teen. Although these young people *can* read, they often choose not to because there are so many alternatives to reading books, including TV, movies, DVD, CD, video games, the Internet, and more. Although the *Book of Hope* for First World youth has been designed in the most engaging packaging and with a special emphasis on the needs of these youngsters, if they choose instead to watch TV or play video games, then the printed *Book of Hope* cannot reach them.

We believe that God's Word has the destiny-shaking power to transform the lives of children and youth completely, but only if it is read and understood. If the alliterate never open the book, it can't help them. Unless we give them God's Word in a highly visual and entertaining format, they may never receive it. There are 280 million children and youth in the First World nations of the world that could be considered alliterate.

4. Inaccessible

There are 400 million children in China alone who may attend school and be able to read, but at present their government will not allow a Scripture book to be distributed in the schools. Some Russian believers are able to take the *Book of Hope* across their borders and into China, but it is a comparative drop in the bucket of what needs to be done there. And China's children represent only a portion of the 586 million children and youth around the world who live in nations where we are prohibited from distributing the book.

That is over one billion of the world's roughly two billion children and youth who cannot be reached by the *Book of Hope*. (I have deducted the number of pre-readers from the total non-reader category in expectation that most of the pre-readers *will* learn to read). This is a difficult concept to grasp considering that God has placed the mandate upon us to affect the destiny of the next generation by providing the Word for every child and youth in the world. Through no fault of our own, half of our target mission field is inaccessible to us!

Yet, the Scripture promises, "He isn't far from any of us, and He gives us the power to live, to move, and to be who we are" (Acts 17:28). How can we be who we are — the generation that is going to reach every child and youth with the light of God's love — if there are more than a billion children that the printed Word simply *can't reach?*

God has provided the answer in a character-generated photo-realistic animated version of the *Book of Hope* that can be broadcast on TV, re-created on CD, DVD and other computer replication technology. It can be distributed around the world, with the potential to reach virtually all of those who, for whatever reason, cannot be reached by the printed *Book of Hope*.

God has provided us with the power to be who we are — the generation that fulfills the Great Commission!

Character-generated (CG), photo-realistic computer animation is exactly what is reaching the next generation today. CG-animation uses the live actions of humans as its base, but then is computer-enhanced for a fascinating 3-D effect. It is currently being used to drive popular video games — from fun learning games for kids to violent war games for teens and adults — secular TV shows, interactive CD's and Internet.

But there is no reason that it cannot be used to present the life story of Jesus to children and youth, in a high-tech animated version of the proven *Book of Hope*. This high-quality, digitally-produced program would perfectly meet the four challenges which have so far been unmet by the printed *Book of Hope*.

1. It will reach those who cannot read.

Currently, national believers carry each *Book of Hope* into the schools of a city and present it face to face to the children, right in the classroom. With our well-established network of churches and an infrastructure that spans over 120 nations, it should be possible to organize these same believers to show the video, CD or DVD version to those children who aren't in school, from village to village, and town to town — even in the refugee camps of nations such as Mozambique. We have the teams in place already. We just need the tool.

Further, the proposed program will be targeted and culturally appropriate to each different national audience. This allows us to customize the presentation, just like our books, to nations, cultures, felt needs, and languages.

2. It will reach those too young to read and everyone in the vital 4/14 Window.

Young children respond to the color, motion and sound of character-generated productions, and they will love watching the life of Christ unfold on TV, VCR, CD, VCD or DVD projection and eventually through streaming video on the Internet. The life-changing message will be obvious to them, even if they cannot read.

Already our existing teams are invited to present at school-wide assemblies as they distribute the printed *Book of Hope*, with kindergarten and pre-school children present. This will provide a way for us to introduce Jesus even to these pre-readers, along with the rest of the children in the critical "4/14 Window."

The animated version also has power to get kids in the 4/14 Window into the Word of God because in those areas where we can distribute the *Book of Hope* in the schools, the video can be simultaneously aired on national TV or released through cinema showings and church showings. This will get students talking about the great movie and learning more about the book on which the animated video was based, so it will actually create excitement and enhance the reception to the printed page for millions. The synergy of the visual and literal will make our entire program more effective.

3. It reaches those who can read, but choose not to.

In fact, it is exactly what today's First World children and youth want: the best possible technology and a fast-moving, captivating visual display. Because God built a production team of believers who also represent the best and brightest of the animation industry, we believe the quality of the program should make it possible for the animated *Book of Hope* to be broadcast on the network airwaves of the USA and other nations.

One reason there is so much interest in this project is the great production team God assembled. Our producer is Jeff Holder, a wonderful believer who has served as Vice-President of Production and Programming for Hanna-Barbera, Director of Children's Programs for ABC, and as Sony/Wonder's Vice-President of Creative Affairs. He had been looking for years for a way to powerfully impact kids through the Hollywood media, and he feels this is it.

Jeff was joined by Bob Arvin and Jake Aguas of "3dBob Productions," along with a host of artists and animators who are leaders in their fields. Bob, for instance, has worked on some of Disney's most popular recent motion pictures, and the effort he and Jake gave us was nothing short of spectacular. I wish everyone could have visited the studios during production. Nothing was taken for granted, and no detail was too small for consideration. Once when I was there, they had an actual campfire blazing, and they were cooking fish, just to be sure they captured the exact right motion and sound for Jesus' preparing a fish breakfast for His disciples on the shores of Galilee.

We couldn't afford, and I don't think we could realistically have bought, the kind of expertise and dedication our team brought to the animated project, and yet these fellow Christ-followers worked for their bare minimum needs, and the partners of the Book of Hope ministry gave so generously to make it a reality. God is at work through you!

4. It will reach those in inaccessible areas.

Take the example of the nation of China once again. Although the government is reportedly hostile toward Christianity, we know that there is a strong underground Christian church in China. These national Christians would be thrilled to have a powerful character-driven version of the Scriptures to show to children. There are 88 million VCD (Video Compact Disc) players in China, and the house churches are ready and able to duplicate and use a digital version of the *Book of Hope*.

The program will be distributed to the house churches of China to use again and again to reach millions of children. This strategy can also be used in Middle Eastern nations and throughout the 10/40 Window.

Eventually, it should also be possible to stream the production via the Internet to kids anywhere in the world who have access to go online, even in politically or culturally restricted countries. This is not a far-fetched idea: statistics say that by the year 2007, more people will be online in China than anywhere else in the world!

Can you believe our awesome God? When He gave us the mission to present His Word to every child and youth in the world, we started with the nations where we knew it would be possible, in the languages we knew it would be easy to translate. In less than two decades, He has opened the doors to literally reaching every child and youth in the world. I call that the power to be who we are … the generation with the light of God, ready to share it with all the world.

The story is still being told!

Every afternoon, a nine-year-old boy named Absalom in the African nation of Swaziland takes the bus 42 kilometers to the hospice. He goes to visit his mother, who is dying from AIDS, like so many hundreds of thousands across Swaziland. He reads to her from the *Book of Hope*. Because they have accepted Christ as Savior, Absalom and his mother now know that even if death should separate them, they will one day be reunited in heaven.

In Scotland, Kirsty's mom was a single parent with two teenaged girls to raise, and it wasn't easy. In fact, Kirsty and her friends were at that stage where they wanted to dress in revealing clothes, put on lots of makeup and dance all night at rock concerts. But when a Book of Hope Affect Destiny Team invited them to a Gospel concert at Hope Fest Celebration, everything changed. Today Kirsty, her sister and her mother are all following Jesus!

Imagine – it took just 33¢ each to reach

(over)

Kirsty and Absalom with the *Book of Hope* and transform their lives ... and similar stories are being told in 100 nations around the world, as students are receiving the *Book of Hope* still today. You can help, through your prayers, and through a gift. Every dollar reaches three students with the message of salvation.

Call, write or go online for more information, or to give your gift today!

book of Hope

www.bookofhope.net
1.800.GIV.BIBL (448.2425)
Book of Hope • 3111 SW 10 Street • Pompano, FL 33069

❏ **Please tell me how I can get involved in the *Book of Hope* ministry.**

❏ **I have enclosed a gift, I understand every dollar reaches three children and youth with the *Book of Hope!***

❏ $100   ❏ $50   ❏ $25   ❏ $_____

_____
NAME

_____
ADDRESS

_____
CITY, STATE ZIP

_____
PHONE

_____
E-MAIL

book of Hope

3111 SW 10th Street • Pompano, FL 33069 • 1.800.GIV.BIBL (448.2425)
www.bookofhope.net

Chapter
Ten

Eddie Ogan was a lucky little girl, because she was too young to remember her father's abominable behavior back when she was an infant and a toddler. Her older brothers and sisters did remember. Their mom was loving and kind, but their father was the bane of their existence. He was the stereotypical alcoholic who spent every spare dime on booze, then came home drunk and abusive. He was well-known in their community, Eddie says, as the town drunk. Eddie doesn't remember this side of her father because she was just little when a miracle happened.

It was a freezing cold February night. Eddie's father was out drinking, and sometimes he would get so inebriated that he forgot how to get home, and he would just pass out and sleep wherever he happened to be. But Eddie's mom knew that if he slept outdoors that night, he would freeze to death. She had six children in the house, and she was expecting the seventh, so she couldn't very well go out into the cold and look for him. She had never said a prayer in her life, but that cold, dark night, she knelt beside her bed and prayed, "Lord, if there really is a God, please bring my husband home safe tonight, and I will live the rest of my life for you."

Downtown, Eddie's father didn't know where he was, but he knew it was pretty cold out! He was stumbling drunk and looking for some warm place to crawl into when he saw the inviting lights from an old store-front that had been rented for the evening by an evangelist in town. He wobbled into the service, felt blessed relief from the cold, and collapsed into a more or less sitting position on the very last bench. Even through the alcohol-induced haze, he heard and understood when the evangelist said, "If you don't like what you are, if you want Jesus to change you completely right now, come forward."

Eddie's dad started to totter down the aisle. Some of the believers who had come out to support the visiting preacher were mortified to see the town drunk in their service. They were afraid he was going to embarrass all of them! Someone even called for an usher to hustle him out before anyone noticed, but it was too late. He went to the front of the building and knelt at the make-shift altar. As soon as his knees touched the floor, the effects of the alcohol instantly fled. In his new, sober state of mind, he confessed his sins to Jesus and vowed to make a turnaround in his life. He was instantly cured from alcohol addiction, and then ran the two miles home to tell his wife. She was still kneeling beside the bed praying for him when he burst into the room and shared the good news. Then she, too, confessed Christ as Savior.

The change in Eddie's father was dramatic. Over the next seven years, he went from being the town drunk to being one of the most respected men in the city. Although Eddie was only two years old when the change occurred, her brothers and sisters could remember their father's previous behavior, and they were thrilled by his transformation. He became a charter member of the church, a Sunday School teacher for the adult class, the head of the community's 4-H program, and a member of the church board. And he expressed a great love for his children, and really for all children. All the young people in the community looked up to him.

At age 40, just seven years after he first committed his life to Christ, Eddie's father was called home to be with Jesus.

He had a weak heart, and it finally gave out. On the day of his funeral, all the businesses and schools in two towns were closed, so that everyone could pay their respects to a man who was richly loved.

The death was a terrible blow to his wife and children, but they were so happy over his transformation in his final few years that they stayed strong and steady in their faith.

The family lived on a farm, so money was scarce, and losing their father did not make things any easier financially, as he didn't leave them much. Back in those days, it was especially difficult for a widow to provide for a family of seven children, but with God's light inside them, they happily made do. They did what lots of poor families do: they used cardboard to reinforce their worn-out shoes, they recycled their clothes from brother to brother, mother to daughter and sister to sister, and so forth. They were grateful to God for what they had and thus never considered themselves poor.

After all, Jesus had promised them, "Don't worry about having something to eat, drink, or wear. Isn't life more than food or clothing? Look at the birds in the sky! They don't plant or harvest. They don't even store grain in barns. Yet your Father in heaven takes care of them ... Don't worry and ask yourselves, 'Will we have anything to eat? Will we have anything to drink? Will we have any clothes to wear?' Only people who don't know God are always worrying about such things. Your Father in heaven knows that you have need of all these. But more than anything else, put God's work first and do what he wants. Then the other things will be yours as well" (Matthew 6:25-26, 31-33).

That was enough for Eddie and her family. They would seek God's work first, and He would provide for them.

One day their church announced a fund-raising drive to present a monetary gift to a desperately needy family in the congregation. The pastor wanted everyone to give a sacrificial gift on Easter, and this gift would be given to the needy family. Eddie and her family wanted to give the best gift they could. Their usual routine in order to have money to put in the collection at church was to gather the beer bottles tossed out after the Grange Hall's Saturday night dances — one cent for the small bottles on return, two cents for the larger bottles. But this was something special, and Eddie, her mother and two of the sisters decided they would live on nothing but potatoes for the month of the fund-raising drive, so that their grocery money could go to the poor family. Eddie was old enough to do baby-sitting jobs, and her sister cleaned the neighbors' yards for spare change. They made pot-holders and sold them, and did any little odd job they could to raise money during that month.

On Easter Sunday morning, the day they were to give their sacrificial gift, the family walked to church in the rain, singing together, full of excitement because they had raised $70. Eddie is a senior citizen now, but she still recalls there were three $20 bills, and one $10 bill. They had taken all their change and singles to the grocery store the day before, had it totaled up and changed into these four bills. Wouldn't that poor family be delighted to get this princely gift?!

They placed their gift in the special collection plate that Sunday, thrilled to be able to help a family in need. Later that afternoon, they celebrated with their first real meal in a month, an Easter dinner! As they sat down to eat, there was a knock at the door. Eddie's mom went to answer it, and when she returned, Eddie and her siblings could tell that something was horribly wrong. There were tears in their mother's eyes, and from her hand trailed one of the church collection envelopes. She let it fall lack luster to the table top, and there it spilled out a pile of money: three $20 bills, one $10 bill, and seventeen $1 bills. At that moment, Eddie and her family understood: *they* were the poor family. The church had been raising money for *them*. How humiliating. To add insult to injury, the envelope contained only $87. Eddie, her mother and sisters had raised three-quarters of the money for the poor family — and they *were* the poor family!

Eddie was mortified. She never wanted to go back to church. Now she knew what everyone in their congregation actually thought of her. They thought she was poor, that she needed charity. And worse, they not only considered her poor, but could only spare $17 between them for her! Now she knew they were staring at her faded dress, clucking their tongues over her re-soled shoes. No, she could not go back, ever.

Except her mother said they had to go back. The following Sunday, Eddie and her family put on the best clothes they had, the "good" clothes they always wore to church, and their mother marched them to church, telling them to hold their heads high. What a torment that was, holding her head up and knowing everyone thought she was poor — that this was the "poor family."

That Sunday, a missionary from Africa was visiting the congregation. At least the stories were interesting, and despite her extreme discomfort at being there among those people who looked down on her, Eddie found herself intrigued by the message. At the end of the service, the missionary told the congregation that just $100 would build a church for the tribe he served in Africa. Then they passed around the collection plate. Eddie looked up to catch the twinkle in her mother's eye, and she slowly grinned and nodded her head. Likewise Eddie's sisters and brothers encouraged their mother to take from her purse the fat envelope containing all the money they had worked so hard to raise for the poor family — plus the $17 donated by the other church members — and drop it into the collection.

When the missionary looked at the offering, he was thrilled to see the $87 gift. This was a small church, and these were difficult economic times. A single offering that provided nearly enough to build a church in Africa was a rare event for him, and tears came to his eyes as he exclaimed, "I cannot believe you have given almost $100 from this small church. You must have a very rich family in this church!"

Eddie Ogan and her family had walked into church that morning in their hand-me-down clothes and patched-together shoes as the poorest family in the entire congregation. But in the simple act of giving away what God had placed in their hands, they became the richest family in church. In the span of one church service, they had gone from the very poorest, to the very richest.

Eddie was one of the earliest supporters of the *Book of Hope* in those heady days when we had just delivered God's Word to nearly one million children in El Salvador and begun the march through Latin America, the Caribbean and beyond. Back in those days, each *Book of Hope* could be produced and placed in a child's hand for a cost of roughly 25¢ per student. (Today, some 17 years later, that cost has risen just a little to about 33¢ per child in 2004).

When I unveiled to our ministry partners the new vision to reach all the children of the world with the Gospel in the *Book of Hope*, I had to wonder what the response would be. Most of our friends and supporters had stood by us when we were translating study Bibles into Russian for deprived Soviet pastors, or making evangelistic materials available in Spanish for churches in Central and South America to use on the evangelistic field. Would they stick by me when they heard of this ambitious calling to reach millions of children around the world?

One day I opened a letter from Eddie Ogan, and I feared I had received my reply. She wrote something like, "I have just read about your plan to reach every child in the world with the *Book of Hope*. I did some research at the local library, and around the world today, there are 1.6 billion students — did you know that?"

I held my breath, expecting her next lines to berate me for my audacity, to take me down a few pegs for believing I was the one who could fulfill the Great Commission for the next generation. I feared she would write something such as, "Who do you think you are, Bob Hoskins, to come up with a plan to reach billions?! How are *you* planning to pay for this madness?"

With trepidation, I read on. My eyes filled with tears as I read Eddie's next words. Considering that every dollar provided the *Book of Hope* for four children at that time, she went on to say, "I have enclosed a check for $400. Now all you need, brother Bob, is one million more Christians like me, and you'll have enough to reach every schoolchild in the world with God's Word."

From the very beginning of the *Book of Hope*, partners like Eddie have been the ones who made the difference. I was so touched by Eddie's letter, I shared it with everyone. Just a million Christians who would be willing to give $400 each. Surely there must be one million Christians in the entire world who would be willing to give $400 a piece! From Eddie's startling discovery, we developed a giving club that invited our partners to be "One in a Million" by pledging to give about $400 over the course of a year. To make it simple, we asked them to give the equivalent of one dollar a day, or $365 in a year. Hundreds responded to the call, and from that day to this, have faithfully given $365 each year, and each year we recruit new members to this growing movement.

Eddie's start toward organized giving in order to reach a certain level of number of children each day and each year has grown by leaps and bounds, in sophistication, and in its scope. Today, we have friends who have set lifetime goals of reaching 100,000 or even one million children. Yet it began with Eddie and her vision of being one of the one million to give $400 and reach 1,600 children, .00001% of all the schoolchildren in the world! All we need are one million more like her.

When Eddie sent that $400 gift ministry, her husband caught the vision, too. He said, "I'm a person. I could give $400 as part of the one million people." So he saved and soon sent his $400 gift as well. Hundreds of others joined in this potential army of one million Christians to reach every schoolchild in the world with the Word of God, and Eddie's six grandchildren wanted to help, too. They started saving their quarters — and nickels and dimes, too. In the grocery store, if Mom asked them whether they wanted a candy bar, they would say, "No, just give me the quarters for the Bibles."

The Northwest District of the Assemblies of God was having a coin drive to raise money for the *Book of Hope* in Russia, and Eddie had explained that the money would give Scriptures to Russian children who had never been able to have a Bible before. During that month of the fund-raising drive, the six grandkids raised enough money themselves to give the *Book of Hope* to 500 Russian students. "We'll have enough for 1,000 kids next year," they vowed, and began saving right away.

Eddie's son had three little girls, and her daughter had three little boys. Eddie was leaving on a missions trip for Poland, and her grandsons came from down the street with a last jar of coins for her to add to their collection for next year's coin drive. Then Eddie stopped and spent the night with her son on her way to the airport, and her three little granddaughters gave her their oyster can full of quarters. "I bet we'll have enough to give the Bible to a million kids next year," predicted her six-year-old granddaughter, Kimmy. Only a six-year-old would think she could raise enough money to give the *Book of Hope* to a million students, Eddie thought as she placed the can full of coins in the trunk of her car. She would remember to get it out and add it to the rest of the coins after her missions trip.

But while she was gone to Poland, tragedy struck. The six cousins decided to spend the night together one night, and that night, their house burned down. All six of her grandchildren perished in the flames that night. Eddie knew her precious grandchildren were in heaven with Jesus … but that didn't change the fact of how she missed them and longed to see them and hold them again. Some time later, when she accidentally came across that can of coins in the trunk of her car, it broke her heart again. Here was the legacy of her grandchildren, quarters and dimes in an oyster can.

When the coin drive for the Northwest District began that year, it was made a memorial for Eddie's six grandchildren, who had given so gladly in their quest to give God's Word to the children of the world. It was the largest coin drive ever in that District, and Eddie was on hand when the check was presented for the Book of Hope ministry. She totaled up the amount in her head, and whispered to me, "It's enough for half a million books!" But she had forgotten that it was being presented during our matching challenge. Some friends had offered to give dollar for dollar and match every gift raised at that time. I reminded her that the gift in honor of the grandchildren would be doubled! It would provide the *Book of Hope* for one million children, just as Kimmy had envisioned.

In 1992, Eddie was on one of the Affect Destiny volunteer teams that went to Russia to give the children the one million books that the special offering helped to provide in memory of Kimmy and her sisters and cousins.

Acts 17:27 says that God is not far from any of us. I know God was not far from Eddie's little granddaughter when He gave her the vision of reaching one million children with the Gospel. I believe He was not far from her — in fact, I know He was right there with her — in the flames, on the night that He called her home. He was near enough to welcome her into heaven and say, "Well done, thou good and faithful servant." And Kimmy and her Savior were united together in heaven, as those one million children received the *Book of Hope* in a dramatic memorial to her and her cousins and sisters, whose last act on earth had been to give their best to Jesus.

Participating in the Book of Hope ministry also became a special connection to the memory of their grandchildren for Eddie and her husband. But as you've probably guessed about Eddie now, she's not one to give up, ever. She's not a woman of great financial means, and I don't think she would mind if I told you that it took her eight months to save up that first $400 gift.

One of the jobs they took was cleaning toilets at the county fair. That doesn't sound very glamorous, does it? But Eddie and Phil did it with pride and thankful hearts, because they knew the money they earned would be helping children come to know Jesus. The county officials were so impressed with the Ogans' good work, they invited them each year to clean the restrooms not just at the fair, but also at the rodeo and during "Town and Country" Days. That is hard, dirty work that no one enjoys, but here is what Eddie and Phil have done with that work: for 16 years now, they have donated $1,000 a year, to tell 3,000 children about Jesus, every single year. That is a total of 42,000 children and youth who have received the message of salvation because of Eddie and Phil.

Not everyone understands that kind of compassion and generosity, especially when it requires such hard and nasty work from the Ogans. A friend told Eddie, "I cannot believe you keep doing this work! I wouldn't do that for *any* amount of money."

Eddie answered, "For myself, I wouldn't do it for any amount of money, either. I don't need the money that bad! But to give the Word of God to the children of the world who need to know about Jesus, I do it gladly."

It's a part-time job, three multi-day events per year on top of Eddie's regular job. It's filthy toilets, dirty floors, messy trash and litter. Like Eddie, I wouldn't want to do it for any amount of money. But I also understand why Eddie does it. She has grasped the truth of Jesus' parable in Matthew 25, about the trusted servants who each received a sum of money to invest for their master. The one who received the most invested well and doubled his master's money. The one who received the middle amount did likewise, but the one who received the least just buried his money in the ground, and it never accrued even a tiny bit of interest. Eddie knows that while she may not have been entrusted with a lot of material resources compared to some, she will invest what God gives her wisely in the fields that are ripe to harvest. And I know that she is one of those Jesus will welcome home with these precious words to any believers: "You are a good and faithful servant ... Come and share in my happiness!" (Matthew 25:21).

She is part of the movement to bring the world to Christ, and bring the Word to the world, and together with others like her, she is fulfilling the Great Commission.

Chapter
Eleven

E veryone thinks of time as a progression of events, with a yesterday we can remember, a moment we are living in, and a tomorrow we can plan for. Our lifetime begins when we are born, and ends when we die. The numerous "todays" that make up the actual living are rarely given the weight they deserve, lost in the plodding progression from one moment to the next.

God must regard time in a totally different way than we do, for He has no beginning and no end. His Word says a day is as a thousand years to Him. For Him, the same yesterday, today and forever, there is perhaps no other time but this moment, which stretches from eternity to infinity.

Once in while, maybe once or twice in a lifetime, something happens that forces us humans sideways off the track of linear time into the eternal moment where God exists and radiates time. Such a circumstance is almost always traumatic, for it cuts across every comfort zone and pushes us to the limits of our coping mechanisms.

Most recently, such a trauma made us jump the tracks of time on an early Tuesday morning in September. It was September 11, 2001. Beginning just before 9:00 AM Eastern time and continuing into the following week or so, it seemed to us that time stood still. Everything that usually marked the passage of time for us as Americans stopped completely: the opening and closing of the stock market, the fever pitch of big business, the regular lineup of our favorite TV programs, the specified time for prayer and church-going, the takeoffs and landings, and in many cases, the whining, sniping and arguing.

For a few days, all that stuff didn't seem as important as the horrible tragedy that caught us by the throat and suffocated us. We felt like time was standing still, waiting for us to catch our breath again. And in those days when time stood still, we cast about in our heads for the things that are really, truly, eternally important ... Did I kiss my wife goodbye when I left for work? Did my daughter know I loved her when she left for school? If I had been on one of those planes, is the life's work I would leave behind enough? If I had been in one of those offices, would I have given my life to save another? If I didn't make it out, would I be ready to meet eternity?

That moment of high stakes, all or nothing, now or never, is the moment God lives in eternally, the moment where we, some day, will live with Him, and where I believe He wants all of His children to learn to live, starting now. In the smoldering aftermath of 9/11, those all-important questions were thrust into the everyday prominence they deserve, and made us — whether we wanted to or not — recognize that the extreme *busyness* of our career, our hobbies, recreation and family life, all pale in comparison with the eternal issues of life, death and God. In fact, in light of God and His love for us, *everything* else is just window dressing, mere eye candy for this life that will melt away like a shadow in the sunless daylight of eternity. Says the Apostle Paul, "Christ has shown me what I once thought was valuable is worthless. Nothing is as wonderful as knowing Christ Jesus my Lord. I have given up everything else and count it all as garbage. All I want is Christ and to know that I belong to Him" (Philippians 3:7-9).

On September 11, a friend of our literature ministry called with an urgent request: the traumatized and hurting people madly searching for loved ones in the wreckage of Ground Zero needed spiritual help. Would we send our Scripture books? We gladly rushed 5,000 copies of the *Book of Hope* to be distributed on the streets at Ground Zero. The books flew out of the hands of the volunteers who had come to distribute them and were gone within a matter of moments. Weary rescue workers turned their tear-stained eyes on the book's cover and said, "*Book of Hope? That's what I need. I need some hope.*"

With the response so intense, we readied another shipment of 5,000 more books. Our friends at Times Square Church took the books again to Ground Zero, and again the books were snatched up by people hungry for hope — and the volunteers led 230 people to trust Jesus as Savior, right there on the streets.

That is a real miracle in a big, impersonal city like New York. And I daresay that had the workers of Times Square Church stood out on the streets in front of the World Trade Centers on September 10, they would have had a hard time getting anyone to stop and talk with them or take a book from them. Probably more of those books would have wound up lining the streets and the trash bins than anywhere else. On September 10, time was still passing, still barreling down its relentless progression to tomorrow. On September 10, most people in New York City had no time for God.

But on September 11, when time stood still, the dazed survivors found themselves with nothing but hollow time on their hands, and an aching need to know that there was some meaning beyond the chaos. Sometimes it takes a trauma to force us to focus. If we are wise, we take that moment when time stands still to center our lives on something lasting and recognize for ourselves what matters most.

Maybe human beings can't stand to live in God's eternal moment, every moment. That's just one reason that we so desperately need to learn all we can from those occasions when our concept of time and His are blurred, when our progression of time comes to a halt and we're compelled to look deep into ourselves and our universe for some shred of eternity to cling to.

I think of the nation of Israel, in the book of Ezekiel. For the first 32 chapters of that book, the prophet predicted horrors about to fall on the people because of their disobedience and disregard for God. He tried to show them what was important and pled with them to turn back to the God of their fathers and to recognize the significance of the eternal, but all his words fell upon deaf ears — until chapter 33. There is a marked change in the book of Ezekiel there, a complete turnaround in the attitude of the people. What happened? The children of Israel, living far off in captivity, received a message from Jerusalem: their holy city had been sacked and conquered. Despite their captivity, they had clung to Jerusalem as their symbol of national identity and pinned onto it their dreams of returning to Israel as a unified nation. Now their holy city lay in ruins, and their dreams were dead. Jerusalem had been a monument to their significance, and now it was no more. For the children of Israel that day, time stood still.

Their response was to turn to the prophet and cry out, "If our transgressions and our sins be upon us and we pine away in them, how should we then live?" (Ezekiel 33:10, 21st Century KJV).

I believe this is the defining question of our generation, too. If thousands of people can perish in a moment because of the hatred of an invisible enemy, how should we then live? If two bold monuments to our wealth and ingenuity and the center of our military might can be assaulted so effectively and with such deadly force, how should we then live? If the sky can rain down death on hapless men and women just trying to earn a living at their regular jobs, how should we then live? If there is no guarantee that raising my children right and attending church — even seeking to live my life as close to Christ as I can get — will protect me from the perils that exploded on September 11, how should we then live?

How should we then live? If we have learned anything from the harsh lesson of the day time stood still, we will live as if we have heard the call of God and understand that only what we accomplish for Him is eternal, and therefore important. The Apostle Paul made the point so clearly:

"These little troubles are getting us ready for an eternal

glory that will make all our troubles seem like nothing. Things that are seen don't last forever, but things that are not seen are eternal. That's why we keep our minds on the things that cannot be seen" (2 Corinthians 4:17,18).

Time stood still for us on September 11, and in that moment when we turned ourselves inside-out to rediscover what is really important and what isn't, we should have come up with just this one answer. What is really important is building a legacy for eternity, something we can take with us from this life into the next because this life is brief, but the next one is eternal. For those of us with families and children, that means building God's love into their lives, of course, but it means something more as well, for every child of God. It means fulfilling the mandate that Christ left for us when He bodily exited this world at His ascension.

"Go and preach the good news to everyone in the world," Jesus said in Mark 16:15. "Anyone who believes me and is baptized will be saved" (Mark 16:16).

Today, the Great Commission is far from fulfilled, for there are three billion people who have not yet had an adequate witness to the message that Jesus saves. But I believe the Book of Hope story proves that as a generation of believers becomes galvanized by the possibilities of this age and the power of God, we can be the ones who finally and faithfully carry the light to the ends of the earth. When we do, Christ has promised that we will usher in His triumphant return. When His disciples asked for a sign of His coming in Matthew 24, He gave an extensive list of signs, the most promising of which is this, "When the good news about the kingdom has been preached all over the world and told to all nations, the end will come" (Matthew 24:14).

What a miracle we could be privileged to be part of, if we are the ones to preach the Gospel to all nations. Then we would have the answer for that defining question of our age, "How should we then live?" Our answer will resound:

"We will live like the final generation of Christ-followers, carry the light of His love to every person on earth, and *become* the generation that welcomes Jesus back."

I know the people who are already making it so. They are people like Charles Brinkley, a Vietnam veteran, who is actively involved in reconciliation ministry. He guides groups of vets like himself back to Vietnam, to interface with the people and exchange views, memories, and forgiveness. It is a powerful healing ministry. Charles' heart has naturally been deeply moved for the people of Vietnam, and for years he has wanted to see the children receive the *Book of Hope*. In anticipation of that day, he provided the entire funding for translation and development of the Vietnamese-language *Book of Hope*.

This is possible through our Centurion/First Edition program. I have mentioned that at today's prices, it takes about 33¢ to place the *Book of Hope* into the hands of a needy child. You have probably guessed by now that there are some foundational costs for each new language and version that are not covered in that amount. It is glamorous and fun to be able to say, "Every dollar gives God's Word to three children, so my $50 gift is reaching 150 students!" It's true, too. Once the book is ready for press, an average of just 33¢ per child is spent to print and deliver the book.

But before it gets to that stage, several things have to happen. We have a standard set of Scriptures that we use, modern and easy to understand, and each book must be translated from those Scriptures. Often we also do research among the target age group and country to make sure we are using the best and most effective packaging, and to make sure the extra sections that focus on specific needs apply in that culture, age group, and country. Then those sections also are translated, and the new design is drawn up. The artwork and typesetting must also be created, often from the ground up.

This is not an inexpensive process, and there are two groups of people who help us with it: Centurions, who have committed to give $1,000 annually to pool for the development of the *Book of Hope* in new languages and editions, and those who give to the "First Edition Fund."

It gives me a chill to think about it, and I know it gives Charles and his wife Jeanne a chill, too: as God opens the door to

Vietnam, it helps place the Gospel into the hands of every child in the nation. Here is a guy who was once forced to go and fight against the Vietnamese, who experienced, I am sure, depths of terror and anger that I can't even imagine because I have never been in that situation. Yet out of that horror, God has brought forth an amazing gift for the next generation in Vietnam.

Our Centurions and First Edition Fund investors are people of great foresight and compassion, who give significantly of prayer and resources in order to fulfill the mission statement of this ministry: to affect the destiny of the next generation by providing God's Word for all the children and youth of the world. Maybe God is calling you to do the same?

There are other ways you can get involved, and I have mentioned several in the pages of this book. In addition to giving as a Centurion or investing in a First Edition, you can give to place God's Word into the hands of students: every dollar reaches three children or youth. Or you can join the Book of Hope Animation Guild, which is helping to translate the animated version into new languages and dialects. Further opportunities for involvement:

Affect Destiny Teams

For groups: Affect Destiny Teams leave nearly every week for what are typically 10-12 day mission trips around the world. Teams travel to places like Latin America, Eastern Europe, the former USSR, and Africa to share God's Word. These teams of youth, young adults, singles, and other adults connect with students using drama, illustrations, and stories.

For individuals: Affect Destiny Teams have opportunities for individuals called to share God's Word with youth and children around the world.

- *Affect Destiny Extreme Teams* take God's Word to the world's remote places like Papua New Guinea, the Amazon Jungle, etc.
- *Affect Destiny Single Adult Ministry Teams* consist of single adults wanting to share God's Word throughout the world.

- *Affect Destiny Extended Teams* consist of individuals who minister together for 3-6 weeks in places like Africa, South America, Eastern Europe and Oceana.
- *Affect Destiny Internship* opportunities exist for ADT alumni who seek a longer (approx. 4 month) discipleship journey through time in South Florida and ministry throughout the world.

For more information, call the office at 800.448.2425, or check out our Web site at www.affectdestiny.net.

Book of Hope Response Team

Our full-time missions staff, the Book of Hope Response Team, consists of missionary associates available for use in numerous ways to carry out the vision of Book of Hope. Through leading Affect Destiny trips, training Affect Destiny Teams, RT members play a big role in sharing God's word with all the youth and children of the world. Typically, members are accepted to join RT after graduation from our internship program, or experience on the international mission field or in local churches.

For more information, call the office at 800.448.2425, or check out our Web site at www.responseteams.net.

Hand in Hand

Almost anyone can make a simple bracelet out of beads and a leather strap — we'll even provide the materials. We'll send you enough to make 15 Hope Bracelets, and a Book of Hope Bank to save and send $5 in change, enough to provide 15 books. The books and bracelets you send will be given to needy children as we explain the salvation story to them. This is a great project for kids, seniors, women's groups and others.

These are just a few of the ways you can be a part of the Book of Hope Story, and tell children and youth around the world that Jesus loves them.

Chapter
Twelve

I heard of a spinster lady in London who went each afternoon to her favorite little bakery for biscuits and tea. She was so particular about her biscuits that she carried a handbag and always had her personal bag of the cookies she liked best. She always had a book or magazine in her bag, and she had her favorite table. It was a lovely, enjoyable ritual for her. One afternoon, she arrived at the bakery to find it very crowded. She had a difficult time just securing her favorite table, and then when she had it, one of the other customers who was alone seated himself across from her. She didn't like it, but it would have been rude to tell him to leave when the place was so crowded. She tried to ignore him and concentrate on her book. They were each served their pot of tea, and the lady began to eat her first cookie. What a surprise when, after she had taken her first bite, the man reached over into the package of cookies and took one for himself!

The lady was mortified. Here the fellow had sat down at her table without being invited, and now he was helping himself to her special cookies. Still, he was a big man, and she was a little afraid to upset him. She tried to continue with her book and cookies, but as soon as she had her second one, he helped himself to another! And this time, when she gave him a sharp look to communicate her disapproval, he had the audacity to smile at her! Now there was only one cookie left in the package, and her unwanted guest reached into the bag, took the last cookie, broke it, and offered her half. With a peremptory huff, the woman took the half a cookie, gobbled it down, gathered up her things and went to pay for her tea. As she rummaged in her handbag for her wallet, she was shocked to discover her untouched bag of cookies still in place. The biscuits she had been sharing with a stranger weren't her own, but *his*.

Whose cookies are you eating? That is the question for today's generation of American believers. We have churches on every corner, the Gospel on 24-hour TV, Bible bookstores that offer us resources on everything from finding a mate, having a successful marriage, and raising children, to finding fulfillment and growing old God's way. We have stuffed ourselves on the grace of God, and now many of us are still wolfing down the crumbs of salvation that rightfully ought to be passed around to the billions who have never yet had an adequate witness to who Jesus is.

I thank God that there is a movement underway in America and around the world for Christians to back away from the table, pick up the package of cookies, and carry it to the hungry souls who have had nothing yet. Their story is as diverse and exciting as each one who hears God's call. It is the story of a woman on Social Security in Washington who takes part-time jobs so she can give more. It is the story of little children in Sunday School who save their nickels, dimes and quarters so students in other nations can hear the good news. It's also the story of people like the family who helped double the ministry with their gifts back in 1997, and have done so much since then — and David Byker, and Jim Bakke.

David Byker had made a fortune in real estate during the mid-1980's, but when real estate prices plummeted, he and his wife Kathi were left cash-poor with all their money tied up in investments with declining value. They had faithfully supported many ministries, and like other people in their situation, they considered cutting their charitable giving first thing. After all, they were in financial straits — surely God would understand. But when they prayerfully considered what to do, they knew that the ministries were very dear to God's heart. They determined to keep giving.

After that decision, they found that the Lord seemed to be carrying them through the financial crisis, providing just the money they needed, just in the nick of time, again and again. Then David had the opportunity to buy into a profitable company with no money down. Over the next five years, the business tripled in size, and the profits more than tripled. At the peak of the market, David and his partners sold the business for millions. The sale allowed the Byker family to move from supporting the *Book of Hope* to taking an active part in the ministry. They even went with a team to Chita, Russia in 2000 to be part of the celebration of giving the *Book of Hope* to the 100 millionth child to receive it.

Says Dave, "Some people might think all this happened because I was 'smart,' or 'lucky,' but I know it was the Lord's blessing for being faithful."

Real estate broker Jim Bakke would agree. The *Book of Hope* ministry is his story, too. Jim was on an Affect Destiny volunteer team for the first-ever distribution in Russia and our second distribution ever in Honduras, as a sponsor for a team of youth. God impressed him with the power of the *Book of Hope* to change lives on that trip, and his involvement with this ministry has grown since. Now he has set himself a goal of providing the Word of God for one million people in his lifetime. This is an intelligent businessman who has succeeded by the talents God gave Him and by the grace of God ... but when he considered what legacy he wanted to leave, and what he wanted his children to remember about him, he came up with this answer: he wanted to leave a legacy of sharing Jesus with the world, and he wanted his children to remember that his passion was for sharing the Gospel.

I love this idea. Jim works hard every day for his big bag of cookies, but he is not going to sit down and eat them while there are starving people just waiting for a crumb in Africa, Asia, Eastern Europe and beyond. Rather, he is taking those cookies and delivering them in the best possible packaging and the most appetizing appearances to the children who are hungriest for them. What's even better about the cookies that Jim is giving away is that they won't just nourish a hungry body for a few hours. They will nourish a dying soul with the bread of life. When properly ingested and digested, they will save a perishing spirit for eternity.

Many times when believers explain a ministry of evangelism to non-believers (and sometimes to other *believers*), the people respond with some comment such as, "It's all well and good to tell these poor people about Jesus, but wouldn't it be better to feed and clothe them first?" The argument seems to be that no one who is struggling for physical survival can possibly be expected to care about spiritual existence. There are two important answers to this argument.

The first is that we believe in and encourage humanitarian and compassionate aid to the poor and needy. Our volunteer teams often take large shipments of food, clothing or medicine with them when they will be ministering in poor countries. Jesus fed the hungry on several occasions, and He was certainly concerned with healing the sick, so we take our example from Him. We understand that God has called many ministries to feed, clothe and heal the poor and sick. In fact, there are many non-Christian outreaches that do just that, and rightly so.

The second answer to this argument is that Jesus Himself rated spiritual survival far above physical. This is the Man who said it would be better to cut off your hand than to have your whole body sentenced to hell. So considering that God has called the Book of Hope ministry to be concerned with spiritual matters, we cannot rightfully turn from our calling. Jesus said, "What will you gain, if you own the whole world but destroy yourself? What could you give to get back your soul?" (Mark 8:36,37). To Jesus, a healthy body took second place to a healthy soul, and spiritual nourishment took precedence over physical aid. In Matthew 9 when a paralyzed man was brought to Him for healing, Jesus' first response was to say, "My friend, don't worry! Your sins are forgiven" (Matthew 9:2). He knew that the spiritual gift He had to offer far outweighed the physical touch He could convey.

And as for the idea that the funds that place the *Book of Hope* into the hands of children could be better spent on food or clothes for the needy, look at Christ's response to those who thought an expensive offering for Him should have been sold and used to provide humanitarian aid to the poor. It appears in several Gospels:

> *This made some of the guests angry, and they complained, "Why such a waste? We could have sold this perfume for more than 300 silver coins and given the money to the poor!" So they started saying cruel things to the woman.*
>
> *But Jesus said: "Leave her alone! Why are you bothering her? She has done a beautiful thing for me. You will always have the poor with you. And whenever you want to, you can give to them. But you won't always have me here with you."*
>
> Mark 14:4-7

Jesus knew the value of the perfume, and he knew the suffering of the poor. Yet He made it clear that some things are worth more than the physical aid their value could provide. This is the case with the *Book of Hope*. The spiritual value of the Word of God could never be replaced by what its 33¢ per student cost could buy in the realm of humanitarian and compassionate aid. Compassionate aid may keep a hungry person alive physically, but the Word of God can extend eternal life with Christ to them. Humanitarian aid may cure a sick person to live a few more years, but the Word of God can bring them into the kingdom and provide escape from eternity in hell.

Although it may be difficult for us to admit it in 21st Century, post-Christian, relativistic, humanistic America, there is only one way to eternal life. All those who have not made a commitment to Jesus Christ are outside that way and bound for hell. I do not see how we could justify throwing our resources entirely into humanitarian aid to save physical bodies in this lifetime and ignore the much more glaring problem of spiritual souls that will live forever in eternal torment without the intervention of the Gospel.

I don't know what other ministries people like Eddie Ogan and Jim Bakke give to besides the *Book of Hope.* It wouldn't surprise me to learn they sponsor poor children in childcare ministries, or feed, clothe and heal hungry people through healthcare ministries. Those are worthy causes, and I support them myself. But I know if you ask Eddie or Jim where their heart is, it will be in telling people about Jesus and sending them on the way to eternal life. That's why Eddie and her husband have reached 3,000 children with the Gospel every year for the past 16 years. That's why Jim has set himself a lifetime goal of reaching one million people.

When he shared his goal with Rob and me, it started a little chain reaction. What if we could help other people with similar goals keep track of just how many students they had reached with the *Book of Hope?* That way, when Jim wanted to show his children his heart, he wouldn't take them to some plush offices or show them a healthy balance on a ledger sheet. Instead he could take them to the Book of Hope Web site (www.bookofhope.net) and show them the number of students who had received God's Word because he had generously given of the resources God provided. What a joy that would be! Rob and I both wanted to set our own goals and be among the first to get into this special program.

The current cost of each *Book of Hope* is 33¢ per student, so each dollar gives God's Word to three students. Our vision for this program is that you would be able to go to the Web site, log in for your personal account (that will be password-accessible only to you), and write in the goal for the number of children you want to reach this year, in the next five or ten years, or in your lifetime. Then each time you send a gift to Book of Hope, we would update your account to show how many children have been reached. During special giving events, like our annual matching challenge, you will even see that your giving is doubled during that time, because the challenge fund will match every gift you give. This is a staggering concept, being able to see from day to day exactly how many children and youth have received the good news of Jesus, because of your generosity.

Even if you don't use this Web tool, there is still a way for you to track in general how many children and youth have received the *Book of Hope* through your giving: just keep track of how much you give (you can place the *Book of Hope* into the hands of three students for every dollar you give). For some, that might mean giving $10 a month so they can reach a child every day. For others, it's $1,000 a month to reach 100 every day. I can't get too caught up in the numbers here, but I want to show you that this is the kind of movement God is sparking among His people in these incredible moments of human history. This is the opportunity He has given you and me as His ambassadors to carry His Word to the ends of the earth.

He has filled up our sack with the best, most delectable cookies ever, and given us the most effective and wonderful way to hand these cookies out around the world to every hungry child and youth, and even keep track of how many we have fed with the precious bread of life. We just have to be willing to cast our bread (or cookies!) upon the water. We don't want to be eating the Savior's cookies and then keeping for ourselves the ones He has provided for us to give to others. We want to nourish all the hungry souls we can by the power of His hand, because when we do, what we are really saying is: "Come Lord Jesus!" We are showing God that we have united as the last generation of believers before the return of the Lord, and we want to be the ones to welcome Him when He comes back for the saints.

Jesus' disciples asked Him, "What will be the sign of your coming and of the end of the world?" (Matthew 24:3). Jesus replied that there would be false messiahs, wars and rumors of wars, starvation, earthquakes, persecution of believers, the spread of evil and the rise of false prophets. Then He declared, "When the good news about the kingdom has been preached all over the world and told to all nations, the end will come" (Matthew 24:14).

Never before in history has any other generation had the potential to actually preach the good news about the kingdom all over the world. This is our moment, and this is our time. How fortunate we are to have been chosen to be part of this historic generation!

Chapter
Thirteen

Years ago, a young Romanian girl lay in bed, dying from a heart problem. The cruelty of her condition was not only that it was fatal, but that it caused her to be weak and sickly, so that her last days on earth could only be spent confined to her bed, waiting for death. To get up and pursue any of the normal exploits of youth would surely have killed her that much sooner. In place of a normal young adolescence with friends, boys, clothes and fun, she had only her books. Her favorites were romantic fantasies that transported her into the lives of beautiful heroines and united her with the handsome and charismatic heroes of her dreams. When someone gave her a little picture book about the life of Christ, she set it aside. She felt she was too old for a picture book!

But something about the little book kept calling to Cami from its place on the shelf. One day when she had exhausted her current supply of romance novels, she decided to take a look at the Scripture book. She found that in addition to the pictures, there was a Biblical text that told the story of Jesus. As she read the words, Cami began to wonder if the story was true — it certainly had more substance than her romantic fantasy stories, and something seemed to tell her that it was different in other ways as well. As she read about Christ's power to heal, her own faulty heart began to beat a little faster. If this story were true, could Jesus heal her, too? By the end of the book, Cami was determined to find out all she could about Jesus, and if it turned out that He was real, she wanted to live for Him!

Cami gave her life to Christ, and God miraculously healed her fatal heart condition. She grew up to marry an American missionary to Romania, and for years she passionately told her story as she and her husband carried the *Book of Hope* into schools across Eastern Europe. Children and teenagers understood and believed her because when she told her story, they could easily picture themselves in her place.

Since we began the development of the animated version of the *Book of Hope*, we have become so thankful for men like Phil Vischer. He is the founder of Big Ideas Productions, the group that brings to you and your family the very popular Gospel TV program for kids, *Veggie Tales*. The premise may seem silly — a bunch of vegetables from the plastic drawer in the fridge come to life and teach Bible lessons through their own experiences. But kids love *Veggie Tales* because it is smart, fast-moving, funny and meaningful. Here is what Phil Vischer said:

"Whoever tells the stories shapes society."

If we let Hollywood tell the stories, then our society will be shaped by secular humanists who advocate immorality and greed. If we let the news media tell the stories, society will be shaped by men and women who by and large are far more liberal-leaning than most adults in mainstream America and who have no interest in traditional religion and spirituality. If we want to shape society by the light of God's Word, then we must be the ones to tell the stories to the children, and to the world.

In Mark chapter four, Jesus said essentially the same thing. Everything comes in stories that nudge the listener toward understanding. That's why we want to tell the story of Jesus to children and youth around the world, through the printed page and through our Web site, and through our animated version of the *Book of Hope.*

And that's why I have told you dozens of stories in this book. I hope that you have been able to picture yourself in each one, and understand exactly what the Word of God means to those who have never had the opportunity to hear or understand it. The Apostle Paul said, "I am proud of the good news! It is God's powerful way of saving all people, whether they are Jews or Gentiles" (Romans 1:16). The King James Version says it is "the power of God unto salvation to every one that believeth." Ephesians 6:17 says, "for a sword use God's message that comes from the Spirit." The King James calls the message "the sword of the Spirit, which is the word of God."

The power of God's Word is something we cannot fully grasp, for it broaches "the revelation of the mystery, which was kept secret since the world began" (Romans 16:25, KJV), the mystery of how eternal life with Christ can be granted to the worst of sinners through a simple confession of faith. Although we cannot hope to comprehend the marvelous grace that makes this possible, we do know that God's powerful Word can reshape lives and transform families. We have witnessed it again and again, just in the pages of this book. One of our favorite Scriptures at Book of Hope is Isaiah 55:11, where the Lord declares:

"That's how it is with my words. They don't return to me without doing everything I send them to do" or in the more poetic King James, "So shall my word be that goeth forth out of my mouth: it shall not return unto me void, but it shall accomplish that which I please, and it shall prosper in the thing whereto I sent it."

God's Word cannot return to Him void. We know that if we give God's Word to students, it will accomplish exactly what God has appointed for it to accomplish. All it takes is the unity of believers to decide today that they will be the ones to deliver that Word to all the members of the next generation that have not yet had the opportunity to hear the good news.

Today, God is calling you to be part of this community, to take seriously His command to preach the Gospel in every nation, and to fulfill the Great Commission. He may be calling you to volunteer for a week-long Affect Destiny Team mission. He may be instructing you to fill Book of Hope Banks and make Hope Bracelets for little kids. He may be calling you to give a summer, a semester, a year or more as part of a Book of Hope Response Team. He may be calling you to set a goal for how many students you can reach with the Gospel in this year, the next 10 years, or in your lifetime.

God could be calling you to some other service. What are your gifts? What are your talents? Miriam Machovec moved to Florida to help us launch the ministry of Affect Destiny Teams. She didn't have any particular skill in that area — no one did — but she has a great personality, a sharp, organized mind, and a willingness to be obedient to God's call. Today, she is an indispensable part of our ministry. Marilyn Baughman engineered the *Book of Hope USA* for the students in America. She was a teacher, so she had that educational background, but she wasn't a lawyer and didn't know if it would be legal or how it could be legal to get the scriptures back in the classrooms of the United States. But she is bright, dedicated and willing to follow God's call. It could be that God is calling you to serve the ministry as a volunteer, too.

Or is God calling you to be One in a Million, like Eddie Ogan, and give $1 a day to reach 1,095 children in a year? Eddie says if she can do it, anyone can. Or is God calling you to be like Jim Bakke and give His Word to a million children in your lifetime? If God has placed it in your heart to do it, then it surely can be done. This is your point in the story to tell your part of it … are you ready for that?

As for the end of the story?

Well, we know the end of the tale, because Jesus has already told it to us. Jesus' stories have a happy ending, and this one is no different. In Mark chapter four, several of the stories ended with fantastic growth, with harvest time, with a "harvest beyond their wildest dreams." One of the stories ended with a tree so tall, strong and sturdy that eagles could make their nests in it. One of the stories ended with a beacon of light set high on a lamp stand, drawing all those in darkness toward it.

The end of our story is in Revelation 22 at the gates of the heavenly city where the crystal river runs from the throne of God, and a tree bears fruit for the healing of the nations, with Christ, the light of that city, who says, "I am Jesus! And I am the one who sent my angel to tell you of all these things for the churches. I am David's Great Descendant, and I am also the bright morning star. The Spirit and the bride say, 'Come!' Everyone who hears this should say, 'Come!' If you are thirsty, come! If you want life-giving water, come and take it. It's free!" (Revelation 22:16,17).

We know the end of the story. When we have fulfilled the Great Commission, we can usher in the return of the Lord, and all will be called to that heavenly city for eternity. But that story is still being written today, and this is your moment to write in your part of it. There is a lot of work yet to be done, just to get us from today into tomorrow, to get us from the vision to reality. What will your role in it be? You know you have to be a giver — that is clearly a mandate for all believers. You know you have to share the Gospel, another simple mandate for every follower of Jesus. How are you going to do it? What part are you going to play? How are you going to fulfill your destiny?

I believe the telling of this eternal story is our destiny, yours and mine. And as more and more believers like you abandon themselves to God's plan, this community of believers will continue to swell and bring about a renaissance in the churches of the United States and around the world. This is our moment, and God has confirmed it by opening the technological pathways that make it finally possible for one generation to fulfill the Great Commission. All things are pointing toward you and me as the destiny-shakers and mandate-fulfillers who will band together to make it happen. It *is* happening right now, but we need you to play the special role God has appointed for you.

This story is still being told, and this is your time to tell your part of it. If you want to be part of this storytelling, if you want to share the light of Christ with the millions still suffering in spiritual darkness, then don't wait any longer. Jump into the movement and let the momentum carry you today. There's a praise chorus that says:

The river of God sets our feet to dancing.
The river of God fills our hearts with cheer.
The river of God fills our mouths with laughter,
And we rejoice, because the river is here.

The river is *here*. We are *already in* that holy city. The anointing is upon us right *now*. The light is already burning within us. Jesus said to the crowd in the temple, "The Spirit of the Lord is on me, because he has anointed me to preach good news to the poor. He has sent me to proclaim freedom for the prisoners and recovery of sight for the blind, to release the oppressed, to proclaim the year of the Lord's favor … Today, this scripture is fulfilled in your hearing" (Luke 4:18-19,21,NIV). The Spirit was already upon Him. That same Spirit is *already* upon you. Romans 8:11 says, "God raised Jesus to life! God's Spirit now lives in you, and He will raise you to life by His Spirit."

There is nothing more to wait for. You've received your anointing, received your calling, received your command from the lips of the Savior Himself, "Go and preach the good news to everyone in the world" (Mark 16:15). All that is waiting is for your response, for you to tell your part of the story, for you to play the role appointed to you, and fulfill the destiny God intends for you. What greater joy could you hope to possess than to stand before the Father having fulfilled His objective for your life?

Once upon a time, the Father of light switched on His eternal light inside you, and set you down on this earth to shine. The rest of the story is up to you.

For more information, contact us at:
Book of Hope
3111 S.W. 10th Street • Pompano, FL 33069
www.bookofhope.net • 800.448.2425
info@bookofhope.net